## Also by W. S. Merwin

# SIR GAWAIN AND THE GREEN KNIGHT

# SIR GAWAIN AND THE GREEN KNIGHT

*a new verse translation by*

## W. S. MERWIN

ALFRED A. KNOPF · NEW YORK

2005

THIS IS A BORZOI BOOK
PUBLISHED BY ALFRED A. KNOPF

Copyright © 2002 by W. S. Merwin
All rights reserved under International and
Pan-American Copyright Conventions.
Published in the United States by Alfred A. Knopf, a division of
Random House, Inc., New York. Distributed by
Random House, Inc., New York.
www.randomhouse.com/poetry

Knopf, Borzoi Books, and the colophon are registered trademarks of
Random House, Inc.

Portions of this work were originally published in
*The New York Review of Books.*

Grateful acknowledgment is made to Oxford University Press for
permission to reprint the transcription of *Sir Gawain and the Green
Knight* edited by J. R. R. Tolkien and E. V. Gordon, second edition
edited by Norman Davies (2nd edition, 1967). Copyright © 1967 by
Oxford University Press. Reprinted by permission of Oxford
University Press, Oxford, England.

Library of Congress Cataloging-in-Publication Data
Gawain and the Grene Knight. English & English (Middle English)
Sir Gawain and the Green Knight : a new verse translation / by
W. S. Merwin.—1st ed.
p.    cm.
ISBN 0-375-70992-4
1. Gawain (Legendary character)—Romances.  2. Arthurian
romances.  I. Merwin, W. S. (William Stanley), 1927–  II. Title.
PR2065.G3 A35 2002
821'.1—dc21          2002020281 5

Manufactured in the United States of America
Published October 15, 2002
First paperback edition, April 2004
Second paperback printing, August 2005

*For Paula*

# FOREWORD

The story of Sir Gawain and the Green Knight that has survived into our day in this poem had been told in different versions for many years, perhaps for centuries, before it reached the form that we have now. Foreshadowings of it may have existed in folk tales, and earlier variants of parts of it had been written in tales and romances, many of them as segments of the growing cycle of Arthurian legend that evolved through the later Middle Ages. Many of the earlier narratives have been lost. Some of them, no doubt, were no longer current by the time the author of the present poem, whoever he or she may have been, put it into the form and words that have come down to us.

We do not know the poet's name, and cannot say for certain when the poem was composed. All we have is internal evidence from a single manuscript that was found, early in the nineteenth century, by J. P. Gilson of the British Museum. It had been in the library of an Elizabethan bibliophile, Henry Savile (1568–1617) of Yorkshire, and had been acquired by a later collector, Sir Robert Cotton.

The manuscript (now known as MS Cotton Nero A, Art. 3) contains three other poems, all in the same fine, precise, slightly ornate script. Scholars believe that the writing dates from around 1400. It is the hand of someone used to writing, which suggests a cleric or someone resident in a monastery, or at least trained by priests. The other three poems in the same manuscript, *Purity, Patience,* and *Pearl,* use their stories as vehicles of Christian exhortation and piety. We do not know that the person who copied out the four poems had actually composed any of them, or that they had all been written by the same poet, but from stylistic and temperamental affinities in them, most scholars have concluded that the same gifted person was the author of all of them.

If it was around 1400 that they were written out into one manuscript, either by the author or by a copyist, they must have been in existence for some time before that, through the later years of the fourteenth century, a hundred years before Columbus's fateful voyage. So they may have been written during Chaucer's lifetime, but scholars agree that Chaucer probably never knew any of them. The language of the poems is highly sophisticated, and they display a telling mastery of poetic and narrative form; yet they seem more archaic, more remote from modern English, than anything in Chaucer.

The difference is one of place rather than of time. Chaucer's language and his poetic life were centered in London. The Gawain poem appears to have been written in Cheshire or Lancashire, somewhere near the Welsh marches. The Gawain poet speaks with what seems to be first-hand familiarity of the landscape of North Wales and Wirral, as though his audience would know the region he was talking about. When Gawain rides in search of the Green Knight,

> He has all the isles of Anglesey to the left of him
> And rides across the fords between the headlands
> Over by Holyhead, and out on the far shore,
> Into the wilderness of Wirral, where there were few living
> Who had love at all for God or anyone.

From the scholars' opinion that the same poet wrote all the poems I derive an image of him in later life making a fair copy of what he had written in earlier years. The intimate, grisly knowledge of the hunt and the familiarity with late-thirteenth-century castle architecture and armor suggest that the author was a man, though the *lais* of Marie de France, written in the late twelfth century, should save us from assuming that too readily. In the late nineteenth century there was disagreement among some scholars as to the chronological order in which the poems probably had been composed. They hoped to be able to derive from that progression some understanding of the poet's life. By 1918, when Hartley Bateson published his edition of *Patience,* they were coming to rely on considerations of meter in the different poems to suggest the most plausible order of their composition. They concluded that *Purity* and *Patience,* written in the stressed alliterative line that was a descendant of Anglo-Saxon poetry, were the ones that had been written first.

I discovered *Patience* when I was nineteen (it was not part of any course, which probably added to its attraction), and can remember the pleasure I took then in the tumbling diction and the vivid recounting of the tale of Jonah.

> A wild rolling whale, as fate would have it,
> That was flung up from the abyss, floated by the boat
> And was aware of that man as the water reached for him,
> And rushed to swallow him, opening his maw.
> The others still had hold of his feet and the fish had him,
> Threw him into his throat without a tooth touching him.
> Then swiftly he slips down to the sea bottom.
> Lord! Cold was his comfort and his care huge,
> For his case was clear, and the woe that was upon him:
> From the boat into the wild waves to be snatched by a beast
> And flung into its throat all in a moment,
> Like a mote in through a minster door, so vast were his jaws!
> He slides in past the gills through rheum and slime,
> Spinning on down a bowel that he took for a road,
> On, heel over head, whirling about,
> Until he blundered into a cavern as big as a hall . . .

I had that "mote in through a minster door" in my head even before I knew the other poems in the manuscript.

In *Purity,* with a sumptuous account of Belshazzar's feast, the poet uses description to intensify the dramatic suspense of his story, as he does in the Gawain poem.

*Pearl* is believed to be the last written of the four poems. It is clearly distinct, metrically, from the other three. The verse is still densely alliterative, but the artfully designed poem is cast in rhymed stanzas. The story is an allegory so rich in symbolism that some critics have maintained that the narrative is entirely symbolic, though others have been as sure that it has its source in the poet's biography. It tells of the death of a very young child, the narrator's daughter. She is the pearl with whose loss the poem begins. In his grief the narrator falls into a swoon and begins to dream. He comes to a vision of a garden of unearthly beauty. There, on the far side of a stream, he sees a figure who is both a child and a maiden with a crown on her head. She is his transfigured daughter, and she discourses to him at length on the consolations of Christian faith and eventually allows him a glimpse of her in the heavenly Jerusalem. When he sees her there, he rushes toward her, and wakes.

*Purity* and *Patience* are linked to an earlier English tradition. *Pearl,* with its rhyme schemes and stanzas and dream allegory, is closer to models from France, such as the *Roman de la Rose.*

The Gawain poem is thought to have been written some time after *Patience* and *Purity,* and before *Pearl,* presumably while the poet was still in his mature youth. *Pearl,* unless the story is pure symbolism, suggests that the poet had had a daughter. We can tell from the poems that he read French and Latin and was familiar with Mandeville and the Vulgate Bible. If the Gawain poem was written near the Welsh marches, the poet may have spoken Welsh as well as English.

Yet such biographical speculation is scarcely more than learned guesswork. At the end of *Sir Gawain and the Green Knight* the poet tells us how many stories have been left untold. His own masterful narrative comes late—almost at the end of the evolution of Arthurian tales, romances, and poems that had been welling up from their Celtic sources in Wales,

Ireland, Cornwall, and Brittany throughout the later Middle Ages. They had spread out through Teutonic and then Norman England, onto the Continent, south to the Pyrenees and east to Germany, and back again, through those violent centuries, impelled by an apparently inexhaustible magic whose spell has continued in retellings from Malory to our own day.

Somewhere in the development of that body of legend the source of its enchantment became personified in the figure of Merlin, the great wizard and poet, the representative of Druidic antiquity, of the green world, whose immeasurable presence was depicted standing behind Arthur, foretelling, fostering, directing, and to a degree inventing him. One modern mythologist, Heinrich Zimmer, in *The King and the Corpse,* speaks of Merlin as "not only the master of the forest who entices the chosen one into the field of perilous tests, he is also the founder and guide of the knightly Round Table and the teacher of King Arthur, its lord. In the normal daylight world, that is to say, he calls together the numbers of the elect and then sends them out, one by one, into the darkness to confront the tests by which they are to become transformed. Merlin is the master of the entire cycle—the shapeshifter, the mysterious, benign, yet frightening pedagogue, the summoner, the tester, and the bestower of the ultimate boon."

By the time of the Gawain poet, the fabric of Arthurian legend had come to comprise one of the great bodies of myth and legend known to us, an imaginary world, a metaphoric landscape and history. It is no accident that J. R. R. Tolkien (who, with E. V. Gordon, in 1925 produced the authoritative text and edition of *Sir Gawain and the Green Knight* that I have used for this translation) in time produced his own great modern Arthurian romances, *The Lord of the Rings* and *The Silmarillion.* Tolkien was a great scholar of the Arthurian cycle, a vastly erudite linguist and a born storyteller. He too, in his turn, was enticed and guided by the enchantment of Merlin.

The Gawain poet, long before him, was a spellbinding narrator with a great gift for using cumulative detail to build up the suspense of his narrative and draw its strands together. He told his story so well, in fact, that I would rather not spoil it for any reader who does not know it already in one version or another by giving a synopsis here, though I want to mention a number of things about it. I would like to allow readers new to the story to have their first full encounter with it in the poet's own telling of it.

He has woven together two distinct threads of narrative into one. The first is a mortal challenge, and the other is a tale of erotic temptation. Both are of Celtic origin: Welsh, Irish, or both. There are several earlier forms of the challenge story. One occurs in a Middle Irish narrative, *Bricriu's Feast,* that dates from around 1100. Jessie L. Weston, in *The Legend of Sir Perceval,* tells of a French source of the challenge in a romance originally composed by a Welsh poet named Bleddri, who was famous in his day for his knowledge of the "tales of the British kings and nobles." Another French source, with a Welsh antecedent, may have been *Le Livre de Cardoc,* part of the unfinished twelfth-century *Perceval* of Chrétien de Troyes.

The erotic temptation story has many precedents in Arthurian tales, more than one of them in French romances where Lancelot is the hero, but in two of them, *Hunbaut* and *Le Chevalier à l'épée,* the hero is Gawain. The Gawain poet may have known antecedents of different parts of his story in several languages. He speaks of having heard his Gawain tale "in the hall," told or sung by a minstrel, whether we are meant to take that literally or accept it as a deliberate archaism, a poetic convention used to invoke an earlier legendary, heroic time.

That archaism, that "once upon a time" perspective, is a constant, assumed setting in most of the Arthurian tales, part of their spell. It is so thoroughly integrated in them that it is able to enhance and illuminate familiar details of the contemporary life of the narrator and his audience, things such as court rituals, food, the ideals and some of the actual facts of knightly behavior.

In historic time, the Gawain poem was written during the Hundred Years' War, an era of grotesque and all but constant violence between the English and the French, most of it happening in the west of France, while the Arthurian stories traveled back and forth in waves, as entertainment, across the same areas. The campaigns of that century (the fourteenth), in the wake of the ruthlessness of the Crusades, the merciless slaughter of the Albigensian repression, and the establishment of the Inquisition, followed the claims of the French-born or French-oriented Plantagenet kings of England, Henry II and Richard the Lion-Heart. They raged across Normandy, the Île-de-France, and Aquitaine, heading up into battles of hideous butchery, but more often conducted in devastating *chevauchées:* highly armed mounted raids in great force that swept over long arcs of terrain, bringing slaughter, rape, and torture to everyone found there who was not worth taking prisoner, and burning whatever could not be plundered and hauled away.

The looting of France in that century was one of the main incentives that drew the English of all social stations to the ever-renewed wars across the Channel. Many of the great fortunes and estates of England in that period were built from that ceaseless pillage. In terms of strategy, the huge raids were thought of as a kind of total war, meant to weaken an adversary by visiting terror and destruction upon his subjects. Towns, castles, manors were sacked, and the spoils divided, before they were burned, and the raiders sold or sent back to England such obvious forms of wealth as coin and jewels, furniture and animals, loading the plunder on barges. Hostages—sometimes the most important plunder of all— were held for ransom. Almost any prisoner might fetch something; and some, indeed, were worth a fortune. Captors sometimes divided the price of important prisoners whom several of them had taken. One English knight's share in a French knight captured in Edward III's 1346 campaign on the Cherbourg peninsula was 1500 pounds. After that expedition and its raids, Froissart wrote, in Caen, that the King "sent to England his navy of ships loaded with clothes, jewels, vessels of gold and silver, and other riches, and of prisoners more than 60 knights and 300 burgesses." This, along with the wholesale, reckless, indescribable cruelty of the raids, was part of the reality of warfare, the background against which the romances were written and told and read, and the knightly ideals continued to evolve.

The chivalric point of view, which served to glorify and, literally, to romanticize this tirelessly indulged appetite for robbery and murder, was well established during the first generations of the Plantagenets. Aliénor—or, as she is most often called now, Eleanor—of Aquitaine, whose life spanned most of the twelfth century, was more gifted, original, and admirable than her first husband, the king of France (Louis VII), her second husband, the king of England (Henry II), and either of her sons who became kings of England, Richard the Lion-Heart and the notorious King John of the Magna Carta. She established a cultural tradition that included much that we think of as chivalry: an imaginative spirit and attitude toward existence that maintained the elaborate codes and manners of courtly love and the criteria for knightly prowess and magnanimity. The ideals and their spirit found expression in the poetry of the troubadours, and for most of her life Aliénor was a preeminent patron and close friend of troubadours. Some of the poetic conventions that had come from the assumptions of chivalry and of courtly love survived not only savage treatment from Aliénor's estranged husband Henry (who destroyed her first Court of Love in Poitiers, in 1174) but their own early forms in the medieval world. The word "roman" was used in the eleventh century for the language of the south of France, the language of the troubadours, which came to be called Provençal, or, more accurately, Occitan. The tales of knightly adventures and amorous encounters came to be called romances. The distant beloved, the loved one scarcely known and yet loved for a lifetime, perhaps the object of all the poems written by a poet, and the hopeless longing for an unattainable beloved, recurred with variations. From their early places in chivalric amatory mores, and in the troubadours' poetry, they were passed on to Italy, to Guido Cavalcanti and Dante and Petrarch, and then to the poets of France, and to the Elizabethans, to the nineteenth-century Romantics, and to much that we mean by the word "romantic" in our own day.

My own interest in the sources of that tradition and its relation to the early troubadours and the origins of their poetry had been with me since my years as a student, and eventually it led me back, by a circuitous route, to *Sir Gawain and the Green Knight*. Aliénor's grandfather Guilhem IX, Duke of Aquitaine, is often referred to as the first of the troubadours. He certainly was a talented poet, a sensual man of headstrong, independent mind; and though he may not have been the first of the troubadours (there is no way of knowing) he was certainly one of the first. He had the position and the means, besides, to encourage what was to become the great current of troubadour poetry and music. His own songs, or eleven of them, are the earliest troubadour poems that have survived into our age, and it is possible to trace their influence on the songs of the generations that followed. What we know of him is revealing not only about the troubadours but about the culture of his age and of the centuries between his lifetime (1071–1126) and the end of the Middle Ages.

In the eleventh and twelfth centuries the poets and the nobility of the Aquitaine and of the domains of the counts of Toulouse looked to Arabic Spain, not to Paris, as the source of the arts and manners and cultivated pleasure. The rulers, and the poets, came to know the civilization of Arabic Spain from long and often seductive sojourns south of the Pyrenees, as friends and allies of the Spanish kings of Aragon and Castile. The relations between Spanish and Arab kingdoms on the Iberian peninsula were not composed of unmixed hostility. The cultures had been living as neighbors for generations. Some Arab kingdoms were protectorates and allies of Christian kings. Many of the knights and nobles of the Aquitaine and Languedoc must have arrived as boorish bumpkins at the Hispanic courts with their Moorish dancers, musicians, comportment, and poetry. Spanish Arab poets, since the ninth century, had written manuals about the refinements desirable in amorous relations, adapting Ovid's *Ars amoris* as one of their sources, but elevating it, treating love as a spiritual devotion—the most famous example was Ibn Hazm's *The Dove's Neck-Ring*. The knights and poets from north of the Pyrenees had further contact with some of the splendors and admirable characteristics of Arab culture, of course, when they went east on the Crusades. The occupation of Antioch and Acre allowed them to see, and come to admire and emulate, the elegance in the arts and manners of their adversaries, and to develop a taste for them.

Much of what they admired and took pleasure in came to be incorporated, in one way or another, in the traditions of chivalry and the conventions of troubadour poetry and music. More than half of Guilhem d'Aquitaine's poems are in stanzaic forms adopted from Arabic poetry, and his lines bring from the same models an element new to European poetry: rhyme.

I had been drawn, as a student, to this astonishing flowering of beauty out of a ground of violence, by the troubadours and what I could grasp of their poetry. Almost anything in the whole of the surviving poetry of the first two or three generations of troubadours could serve as an example, but perhaps nothing better than the opening stanza of one of Guilhem's love songs:

> With the sweetness of the new season
> woods fill with leaves and the birds sing
> each of them in its own tongue
> set to the verse of a new song;
> then is the time a man should bring
> himself to where his heart has gone.

I had been more or less familiar with the early troubadours for decades, when a lifelong reading of Dante, which had begun at the same time, led me at last to try to translate the *Purgatorio,* the part of the *Commedia* that I have long loved best. That brought me back to the troubadours with renewed focus. It was in the *Purgatorio* that Dante gave most scope to the arts and artists he loved, and to the poets whom he recognized as forbears. Readers of modern poetry in English will be familiar with Eliot's dedication of *The Waste Land* to Ezra Pound with the phrase *il miglior fabbro.* The whole verse, in the *Purgatorio,* is *il miglior fabbro del parlar materno* (the better workman in the mother tongue). The poet the words refer to, who is being pointed out by Guido Guinizelli, a revered Italian predecessor of Dante's, is Arnaut Daniel, whom the Guido of the poem, and so presumably Dante, regards as the greatest of the troubadours. The reference is an indication of how intimately Dante and his Italian predecessors knew the troubadours and their language, and although sometimes the *parlar materno* has been assumed, rather thoughtlessly, to be Italian, that is unlikely, since Arnaut Daniel did not write in Italian but in Occitan. Beyond that, the *parlar materno* must be poetry itself.

In his poem, Dante places Arnaut Daniel at the end of Canto XXVI, among those whose sin is carnal love, a position he might have earned through his eminence in troubadour love poetry with its erotic assumptions, if nothing else. And Dante, in that passage of his own poem, accords to Arnaut Daniel a supreme gesture of respect and gratitude. When Dante, the pilgrim on the mountain, has addressed the burning shade of the troubadour, Arnaut answers him, not in Italian, but in the language of his own poetry, Occitan, in verses that echo poems of Daniel's that Dante would have known by heart. The eight lines of his reply are among the most beautiful of the entire *Commedia.* (It was this canto of the *Purgatorio* that I first tried to translate.)

When Guido Guinizelli points out Arnaut Daniel to Dante as *il miglior fabbro,* he says of him:

> verses of love and stories *(prosa)* of romance
> he was peerless in all of them

Besides his celebrated, linguistically and metrically dazzling poems, Daniel was well known for his romances, and particularly for one about the love of Lancelot and Guenever. There were several romances about the legends of Lancelot and Guenever in the generations before Dante wrote, but some Dante scholars have been convinced that the one Paolo and Francesca were reading, in Canto V of the *Inferno,* the story that awakened them to their love of each other, was Daniel's, which was lost long ago, along with all of Daniel's other *prosa.*

Before Arnaut Daniel's generation, Bernart de Ventadorn (circa 1120–1190), another great troubadour—some would say the greatest of them all—and one who, like Dante, made love his single theme, directed the envoy of one of his last great songs to a friend, perhaps a singer, to whom he gave the code name of Tristan. Daniel's lost romance, and Bernart's use of the legendary name from the Welsh story, were indications of the degree to which the current of Celtic myth had been made familiar, by minstrels and storytellers, and through written manuscripts, in the castles of Aquitaine and the domains of Toulouse, by the time of the first troubadours, at the end of the eleventh and the beginning of the twelfth century. The Tristan and Iseult story and something of the Arthurian legend were known, in that region, to the same listeners who were captivated by the manners, music, erotic conventions, and poetry of Arabic Spain, and both currents mingled in the nascent traditions of the troubadours and of courtly love.

All of it, almost at once, was carried north into Normandy and the Île-de-France, and then to England, in what must have been a moment of great cultural excitement. The chivalric tradition in its turn came to influence the Arthurian legends, and the resonance echoed back and forth, from language to language, across the Channel, through the following centuries. I turned back to the Gawain poem, written some two hundred years after Daniel's romance of Lancelot and Guenever, and Bernart's use of the radiant name of Tristan, to look again at a finished Arthurian romance when that cycle of stories had traveled so far and had made its way back once more to the land and to the sound of the language of its origin.

One great medieval scholar, G. L. Kittredge, was convinced that the Middle English poem that we have was based on a French romance that has been lost. The story as we know it now had passed from original versions, perhaps in Welsh, into the Romance languages, and then back to the Welsh marches at the end of the fourteenth century.

The Gawain poet, that late in his tradition, had made use of it in a manner that was at once mature and original. As a student I had approached the story through commentaries and analyses of its themes— the challenge, the testing, the rituals of passage. I had read, or read at, various translations, and had spent enough time and study on my copy of Tolkien and Gordon's edition of the poem, looking up word after word in the glossary, for the volume to be dog-eared and falling apart. And yet I realized that I could not say I had really read it. The Gawain of the poem had even become blurred, in my recollection, with memories of the Gawain I had first read about in children's books about the knights of the Round Table, with the Gawain of Tennyson's *Idylls,* and with figures in Malory. Random reading, over the years, had brushed in some of the context of the Arthurian legend, yet the various layers of the tradition were indistinct, and this time I wanted not just to study the poem but to read it. The translations had not given me a sense of a poem that had once held the attention of an audience in the great hall, many of whom already knew the story in one form or another. I began to try to turn the poem, line by line, into the English I understood, hoping in that way to get closer to what it was like. I was doing it for myself, to begin with.

The Gawain poet's language and his verse are inevitably contrasted with Chaucer's, whose vigor, splendor, and elegance are inseparable from his rhythms and meters, above all his newly adopted iambic pentameter. The Gawain poet's lines, with their alliterated, stressed meter, are characterized by their energy and the dramatic, musical repetition of stressed sounds. His verse seems closer to oral poetry than the metrical forms that were about to succeed it. It demands to be heard, and I feel sure that it must have been read aloud in the poet's own time.

The rhymed "bobs" at the end of each section may be a nod in the direction of something that was coming in—rhymed, metrical verse, to which the poet would turn with very different effect later, in *Pearl*. But they may also be a link to Celtic, particularly Welsh, narratives of the earlier Middle Ages in which sections of prose were rounded off in a few lines of verse, giving the story a formality of pace, and a setting for emphasis or perspective. As I translated I wanted to keep what I could of the movement of the lines, what I felt as their vitality and rush, their pitch and momentum, and to keep an alliterative recurrence of sounds that would echo in modern English the stressed alliterative patterns of the original. I did not want, though, to cramp and twist the lines in an effort to make an exact replica of a verse form in what has become, in six hundred years, another language. And for every reason I wanted to keep as close as I could to the meaning of the original words, so as not to mislead my first reader—myself.

As I tried to hear something of the poem, line by line, I came to notice, or imagine that I noticed, in the fullness and articulation of the diction, the hint of an accent that seemed familiar. Something of the kind had happened years before as I read and reread passages of David Jones, particularly his late fragments in *The Sleeping Lord*. What I thought I was overhearing was an intonation that I recognized—though it had never been mine—from my childhood in the mining city of Scranton, Pennsylvania. There, above my head, I had heard among my elders the sounds of the Welsh language and the intonations of the Welsh accent in English. This was something to which I accorded no importance, nor indeed any interest at the time, and certainly I never supposed then that there was any connection between the stories of Arthur and the Round Table that I read at home and at school—indeed, as often as not they were told as though they had happened in *England*—and the accent that I knew from Welsh churches and in the shops along Main Avenue and on the streets, and from my piano teacher, Ivor Price, and my father's minister friends, the Reverend Thomas Tyvian Williams and the Reverend R. J. Richards with the beautiful, willowy, long-haired daughter named Gwyneth. No one around me at the time ever suggested that the accent, and the language it came from, had anything to do with the latter-day, predigested versions of the Arthurian stories that I encountered then, and my sense now of a far-off suggestion of that intonation in the lines of the fourteenth-century poem written on the edge of north Wales may be purely subjective and imaginary, but I know it must have influenced the way I heard the lines in translating them.

Though we know little more about the Gawain poet than his century and his country, the poem is evidence that he once lived and breathed. And behind the legendary Arthur there was an actual king of Britain, eight hundred years before the poem was composed, who fought the Saxons to a standstill at the end of the fifth century. The knights of the Round Table also had evolved from the warriors mourned in Aneirin's great litany of elegies *The Gododdin,* written after the battle of Catraeth, some time between A.D. 580 and 600, in what is now Scotland. Some of their names—including, perhaps, Gawain's—before they were transformed in legends, are there in sections of the poem such as this one:

> They charged as they rushed to be fighting
> they were drunk with pure mead their lives were short
> Mynydawg's men who won fame as warriors
> for their fill of mead they laid down their lives
> Caradawg and Madawg and Pyll and Ieuan
> Gwgan and Gwiawn and Gwyn and Cynfan
> Peredur with steel in his fist Gwawdur and Aeddan
> where the fight swirled they stood firm and smashed shields
> and though death bore them down they dealt it again
> not one of them returned to what he knew . . .

Merlin himself (no Arthurian tale is complete without a glimpse of him or at least of his influence) had an historic forbear. There may even have been two of them, who came to be merged in a single legend. A few great prophetic poems by one of them have survived. Yet after centuries of study and speculation the historic figures seem to be as elusive and illusory as the fictions that continued to emanate from them long after they had disappeared.

But historic antecedents have only a remote bearing on a great fiction such as this one. Other personages, such as the ancient enchantress Morgan with her vast subterranean influences, and Guenever, Arthur's queen, and heroine of adventures and temptations of her own, are part of the fixed cast of characters of the Arthurian body of legend, and readers or hearers of the poem would have been expected to know who they were as soon as they were named.

It is not references such as these, though, that give the poem its power and authority. It is the insistent presence of the unknown, all the way through, that does that, as it draws the story forward. What are we recognizing, what kind of reality do we ascribe to the great castle in the forest, appearing promptly, in answer to a prayer, on Christmas Eve, and its suddenly revealed proximity to the Green Chapel, which no one in that whole wilderness said they had heard of until then? Who is the beautiful siren, the lady of the castle, the temptress of the third section of the poem? What are we being shown in the three days of grotesque, excited slaughter (which one translator describes as "joyous . . . sheer delight . . . physical sport at its best . . . innocent"—and for all we know the poet himself may have regarded the organized mauling and murder of living creatures in that way, even as he shows us the panic and pain and describes the screams of the wounded) set up in artful contraposition to the scenes of seduction behind the curtains of Gawain's ornate bed?

Above all, who is the Green Knight? The question leads us through the whole poem and is inseparable from the spell of the tale. And in the end, what do we really know about him? Why, indeed, is he green (literary predecessors of his included figures who were gray or black), and how did he come to be so? His own eventual explanation of who he is, toward the end of the poem, seems perfunctory and inadequate, more dubious than his presence had been at any point up until then. The poet's creation of him eludes and mocks latter-day efforts to explicate and interpret him, to say what he might represent, and extract from him his "meaning." Which is not to say that he has none, but only that it is not separable from his disturbing figure.

"Where shall I find you?" Gawain asks, before the end of their first meeting. "Where is your place?" The Green Knight promises to tell him that later, but when Gawain next asks him he simply urges him to "search carefully . . . until you find me . . ."

> Many men know me as the Knight of the Green Chapel,
> So if you ask, you cannot fail to find me.

Yet when Gawain sets out, in due course, to look for him, without knowing where to begin his solitary search except in the wildest and least explored region he comes to, no one has ever heard of a green knight or a green chapel. When he has at last discovered them—or they have appeared to him—and the Green Knight tells Gawain his name, we seem to know less about him than before, and the name seems to restrict him, to remove a dimension, to be a patch out of a poorer illusion, and less credible than the unnamed figure of the story. Is he, perhaps, after all, Merlin himself (more than one commentator has suggested it)? Merlin's powers underlie and antedate those of Morgan or of any other character in the legend. What does the form of the Green Knight's spell—his looming appearance, his challenge, his later emergence—tell us about the power of this giant vision whose voice in the great hall of Camelot at Christmastime created "a silence like death," and who towers over the story from the moment he is seen, giving it its unflagging urgency, its undertone of dread, and who summons Gawain, that paragon of knighthood and courtly love, far beyond anything he thinks he knows, and sends him home at last with his life granted to him, and successful in the eyes of the world, but forever humbled in his own?

In the figure of the Green Knight the poet has summoned up an original spirit with the unsounded depth of a primal myth, a presence more vital and commanding than any analysis of it could be. Is he the Green Man of the forest, a descendant of Druidic tradition and of giant forbears as far back as Huwawa, the Keeper of the Forest in the Gilgamesh epic? Is he the Great Terror, or Death in Life, whose wife is Life in Death? He may be all of them, and finally none of them, or anything so neatly designated. We seem to recognize him—his splendor, the awe that surrounds him, his menace and his grace—without being able to place him, which I think is something that attests to the authenticity of the poem, and the power of a great story. We will never know who the Green Knight is except in our own response to him. At this date there seems to be a kind of extended metaphoric consistency in the fact that we do not even know the poet's name.

I want to express my thanks in particular to Nicholas Howe for his care in reading this translation and his helpful suggestions, though any remaining departures from the sense or spirit of the original must of course be ascribed to shortcomings of my own.

# SIR GAWAIN AND THE GREEN KNIGHT

# I

Siþen þe sege and þe assaut watz sesed at Troye,
Þe borȝ brittened and brent to brondez and askez,
Þe tulk þat þe trammes of tresoun þer wroȝt
Watz tried for his tricherie, þe trewest on erthe:
Hit watz Ennias þe athel, and his highe kynde,                5
Þat siþen depreced prouinces, and patrounes bicome
Welneȝe of al þe wele in þe west iles.
Fro riche Romulus to Rome ricchis hym swyþe,
With gret bobbaunce þat burȝe he biges vpon fyrst,
And neuenes hit his aune nome, as hit now hat;              10
Tirius to Tuskan and teldes bigynnes,
Langaberde in Lumbardie lyftes vp homes,
And fer ouer þe French flod Felix Brutus
On mony bonkkes ful brode Bretayn he settez
              wyth wynne,                15
      Where werre and wrake and wonder
        Bi syþez hatz wont þerinne,
        And oft boþe blysse and blunder
        Ful skete hatz skyfted synne.

Ande quen þis Bretayn watz bigged bi þis burn rych,       20
Bolde bredden þerinne, baret þat lofden,
In mony turned tyme tene þat wroȝten.
Mo ferlyes on þis folde han fallen here oft
Þen in any oþer þat I wot, syn þat ilk tyme.

# I

Since the siege and the assault upon Troy were finished,
The city destroyed and burned down to embers and ashes,
And the man who made the decoys that deceived them
Was tried for his treachery, though no man on earth was more true,
It was the noble Aeneas and his high-born kin
Who came to conquer provinces and become the lords _expasihun_
Of almost all the wealth of the Western Isles.
Noble Romulus went to Rome at once.
Proudly he set up that city at the beginning,
Giving it his own name, which it bears to this day.
Ticius to Tuscany, to begin building there.
Longobard builds high houses in Lombardy,
And far across the flood from France Felix Brutus
Is happy to settle the many hills and the whole breadth
       of Britain,
    Where war and woe and wonder
    Have been known frequently,
    And by turns bliss and despair
    Have changed places suddenly.

And when this Britain was built by this noble knight,
Bold men were bred in it who loved fighting,
And they made trouble in the course of time.
More marvels have happened, often, in this land
Than in any other I know, since that first age.

Bot of alle þat here bult, of Bretaygne kynges,     25
Ay watz Arthur þe hendest, as I haf herde telle.
Forþi an aunter in erde I attle to schawe,
Þat a selly in siȝt summe men hit holden,
And an outtrage awenture of Arthurez wonderez.
If ȝe wyl lysten þis laye bot on littel quile,     30
I schal telle hit as-tit, as I in toun herde,
          with tonge,
        As hit is stad and stoken
        In stori stif and stronge,
        With lel letteres loken,     35
        In londe so hatz ben longe.

Þis kyng lay at Camylot vpon Krystmasse
With mony luflych lorde, ledez of þe best,
Rekenly of þe Rounde Table alle þo rich breþer,
With rych reuel oryȝt and rechles merþes.     40
Þer tournayed tulkes by tymez ful mony,
Justed ful jolilé þise gentyle kniȝtes,
Syþen kayred to þe court caroles to make.
For þer þe fest watz ilyche ful fiften dayes,
With alle þe mete and þe mirþe þat men couþe avyse;     45
Such glaum ande gle glorious to here,
Dere dyn vpon day, daunsyng on nyȝtes,
Al watz hap vpon heȝe in hallez and chambrez
With lordez and ladies, as leuest him þoȝt.
With all þe wele of þe worlde þay woned þer samen,     50
Þe most kyd knyȝtez vnder Krystes seluen,
And þe louelokkest ladies þat euer lif haden,
And he þe comlokest kyng þat þe court haldes;
For al watz þis fayre folk in her first age,
          on sille,     55

But of all who lived here as kings of Britain
Arthur was ever the noblest, as I have heard tell.
So I intend to tell of one adventure that happened
Which some have considered a marvel to behold,
One of the wonders that are told about Arthur.
If you will listen for a little while to my lay
I shall tell it as I heard it in the hall,

   aloud,
  As it is set down
  In a strong story,
  With true letters written
  Together in the old way.


This King was staying at Camelot at Christmastime
With many fair lords and the most beautiful ladies
And the whole high brotherhood of the Round Table
In happy festivity and the high revels of the season.
The men charged in tournaments again and again,
Noble knights jousting in high spirits;
Then they rode to the court and danced to carols,
And the feast went on like that a full fifteen days,
With all the food and entertainment anyone could imagine.
The laughter and merrymaking were a glory to hear,
A happy din all day and dancing at night,
All on a high note in halls and chambers,
With lords and ladies as they liked it best.
They stayed there together with all the wealth in the world,
The most famous knights under Christ himself,
And the most beautiful ladies who ever lived,
And the finest of all was the King holding the court,
All of these fair folk there in the hall
   in their first age,

Þe hapnest vnder heuen,
Kyng hyȝest mon of wylle;
Hit were now gret nye to neuen
So hardy a here on hille.

Wyle Nw Ȝer watz so ȝep þat hit watz nwe cummen,                    60
Þat day doubble on þe dece watz þe douth serued.
Fro þe kyng watz cummen with knyȝtes into þe halle,
Þe chauntré of þe chapel cheued to an ende,
Loude crye watz þer kest of clerkez and oþer,
Nowel nayted onewe, neuened ful ofte;
And syþen riche forth runnen to reche hondeselle,                   66
Ȝeȝed ȝeres-ȝiftes on hiȝ, ȝelde hem bi hond,
Debated busyly aboute þo giftes;
Ladies laȝed ful loude, þoȝ þay lost haden,
And he þat wan watz not wrothe, þat may ȝe wel trawe.               70
Alle þis mirþe þay maden to þe mete tyme;
When þay had waschen worþyly þay wenten to sete,
Þe best burne ay abof, as hit best semed,
Whene Guenore, ful gay, grayþed in þe myddes,
Dressed on þe dere des, dubbed al aboute,                           75
Smal sendal bisides, a selure hir ouer
Of tryed tolouse, of tars tapites innoghe,
Þat were enbrawded and beten wyth þe best gemmes
Þat myȝt be preued of prys wyth penyes to bye,
        in daye.                                                    80
            Þe comlokest to discrye
            Þer glent with yȝen gray,
            A semloker þat euer he syȝe
            Soth moȝt no mon say.

[ 6 ]

The most fortunate under heaven,
The highest King, famous for his will,
Now it would be hard for anyone
To name such a brave host on any hill.

When the year had turned new only the night before
The company that day was served double at the high table.
When the King and his knights came into the hall,
The chanting in the chapel had come to an end
And a loud cry went up from the clerics and the others
Proclaiming Noel once more, calling out the word again,
And then the nobles ran and got the gifts ready,
Called out the New Year's presents, holding them high,
And they debated back and forth over the gifts.
The ladies laughed loudly, all the ones who had lost,
And the winner was not sorry, you can be sure.
All this celebration went on until dinner time.
When they had washed well, they went to sit at the table,
The most famous knights nearest the top, as was proper,
And Guenever, in high spirits, was seated in the middle of them,
In the arrangement of the famous table, with them arrayed around her,
Fine silk, furthermore, in a canopy over her,
Of Toulouse red, and many Tharsian tapestries
Embroidered and set with the finest of jewels
That would have cost a great deal if someone had tried
       to buy them.
      The most beautiful there was the Queen,
      Flashing her gray eye.
      No one had ever seen
      Anyone lovelier in his day.

Bot Arthure wolde not ete til al were serued,
He watz so joly of his joyfnes, and sumquat childgered:
His lif liked hym ly3t, he louied þe lasse
Auþer to longe lye or to longe sitte,
So bisied him his 3onge blod and his brayn wylde.
And also an oþer maner meued him eke                        90
Þat he þur3 nobelay had nomen, he wolde neuer ete
Vpon such a dere day er hym deuised were
Of sum auenturus þyng an vncouþe tale,
Of sum mayn meruayle, þat he my3t trawe,
Of alderes, of armes, of oþer auenturus,                   95
Oþer sum segg hym biso3t of sum siker kny3t
To joyne wyth hym in iustyng, in jopardé to lay,
Lede, lif for lyf, leue vchon oþer,
As fortune wolde fulsun hom, þe fayrer to haue.
Þis watz þe kynges countenaunce where he in court were,    100
At vch farand fest among his fre meny
              in halle.
                  Þerfore of face so fere
                  He sti3tlez stif in stalle,
                  Ful 3ep in þat Nw 3ere                    105
                  Much mirthe he mas withalle.


Thus þer stondes in stale þe stif kyng hisseluen,
Talkkande bifore þe hy3e table of trifles ful hende.
There gode Gawan watz grayþed Gwenore bisyde,
And Agrauayn a la dure mayn on þat oþer syde sittes,        110
Boþe þe kynges sistersunes and ful siker kni3tes;
Bischop Bawdewyn abof biginez þe table,
And Ywan, Vryn son, ette with hymseluen.
Þise were di3t on þe des and derworþly serued,
And siþen mony siker segge at þe sidbordez.                 115

Yet Arthur would not eat until they were all served.
He seemed full of the joy of youth, almost a boy.
He was happy with his life; he cared little
For lying in bed or sitting still for a long time,
His young blood so stirred him and his wild brain.
And there was a custom, besides, that he meant to keep,
That he had assumed in his noble way: he would not eat
On such a holiday until he had been told
A tale all new of some wonderful event,
Of some great marvel that he might believe
About kings, or arms, or other adventures,
Or unless someone came to ask for a proven knight
To join with him in jousting, putting his life in peril,
Risking life against life, each of them allowing
Fortune to grant the advantage to one of them.
This was the King's custom when he was holding court
At every great feast with his noble company
        in the castle.
      So with his proud face there
      Bravely he stands waiting
      Bold in that New Year,
      And joins in the merrymaking.


So the King in his strength was standing there by himself
Talking of court trifles to those at the high table.
There sat good Gawain with Guenever beside him
And Agravaine of the hard hand on the other side of her,
Both of them the King's nephews and famous knights.
Bishop Bawdewyn was up at the head of the table,
And then Ywain beside him, who was the son of Urien.
These were seated on the dais, and lavishly served,
And many renowned knights were near them at the side tables.

Þen þe first cors come with crakkyng of trumpes,
Wyth mony baner ful bryȝt þat þerbi henged;
Nwe nakryn noyse with þe noble pipes,
Wylde werbles and wyȝt wakned lote,
Þat mony hert ful hiȝe hef at her towches.      120
Dayntés dryuen þerwyth of ful dere metes,
Foysoun of þe fresche, and on so fele disches
Þat pine to fynde þe place þe peple biforne
For to sette þe sylueren þat sere sewes halden
                on clothe.      125
          Iche lede as he loued hymselue
          Þer laght withouten loþe;
          Ay two had disches twelue,
          Good ber and bryȝt wyn boþe.

Now wyl I of hor seruise say yow no more,      130
For vch wyȝe may wel wit no wont þat þer were.
An oþer noyse ful newe neȝed biliue,
Þat þe lude myȝt haf leue liflode to cach;
For vneþe watz þe noyce not a whyle sesed,
And þe fyrst cource in þe court kyndely serued,      135
Þer hales in at þe halle dor an aghlich mayster,
On þe most on þe molde on mesure hyghe;
Fro þe swyre to þe swange so sware and so þik,
And his lyndes and his lymes so longe and so grete,
Half etayn in erde I hope þat he were,
Bot mon most I algate mynn hym to bene,      141
And þat þe myriest in his muckel þat myȝt ride;
For of bak and of brest al were his bodi sturne,
Both his wombe and his wast were worthily smale,
And alle his fetures folȝande, in forme þat he hade,      145
                ful clene;

Then came the first course, to the blaring of trumpets
With many brilliant banners hanging from them.
New kettledrums rumbled with the noble pipes
Wakening wild warblings with their loud sounds
And lifting many hearts high with their music.
In the midst of it rare and delicate dishes are served,
Mounds of fresh meat, and so many platters
That it was hard to find enough places
To set down the silver with the stews in it
        on the tablecloth.
        Each one as he pleases
        Takes whatever he will.
        For every two there are twelve dishes,
        Good beer and bright wine both.

Now I will say no more about their service,
For all must know that no one lacked anything.
Another noise and a new one suddenly reached them
In less time than it takes to lift food to the lips.
Scarcely had the sound faded away again,
With the first course in the court properly served,
Than in at the hall door comes a frightening figure,
He must have been taller than anyone in the world:
From the neck to the waist so huge and thick,
And his loins and limbs so long and massive,
That I would say he was half a giant on earth.
At least I am sure he was the biggest of men.
Yet he sat with a matchless grace in the saddle.
His back and his chest and whole body were frightening
And both his belt and belly were trim and small
And all of his features were in proportion
        to the rest of him.

For wonder of his hwe men hade,
Set in his semblaunt sene;
He ferde as freke were fade,
And oueral enker-grene.                                    150

Ande al grayþed in grene þis gome and his wedes:
A strayte cote ful streȝt, þat stek on his sides,
A meré mantile abof, mensked withinne
With pelure pured apert, þe pane ful clene
With blyþe blaunner ful bryȝt, and his hod boþe,          155
Þat watz laȝt fro his lokkez and layde on his schulderes;
Heme wel-haled hose of þat same,
Þat spenet on his sparlyr, and clene spures vnder
Of bryȝt golde, vpon silk bordes barred ful ryche,
And scholes vnder schankes þere þe schalk rides;         160
And alle his vesture uerayly watz clene verdure,
Boþe þe barres of his belt and oþer blyþe stones,
Þat were richely rayled in his aray clene
Aboutte hymself and his sadel, vpon silk werkez.
Þat were to tor for to telle of tryfles þe halue          165
Þat were enbrauded abof, wyth bryddes and flyȝes,
With gay gaudi of grene, þe golde ay inmyddes.
Þe pendauntes of his payttrure, þe proude cropure,
His molaynes, and alle þe metail anamayld was þenne,
Þe steropes þat he stod on stayned of þe same,           170
And his arsounz al after and his aþel skyrtes,
Þat euer glemered and glent al of grene stones;
Þe fole þat he ferkkes on fyn of þat ilke,
            sertayn,
        A grene hors gret and þikke,                      175
        A stede ful stif to strayne,

But more than anything
His color amazed them:
A bold knight riding,
The whole of him bright green.

*meanings of green in this time: nature, envy?*

And all in green this knight and his garments
With a close-fitting coat that clung to his side,
A fine robe over it adorned on the inside
With furs cut to one color, an elegant lining
Trimmed brightly with white fur, and his hood also
That was caught back from his long locks and lay on his shoulders;
Neat, tight-tailored hose of that same green
Clung fast to his calf, and shining spurs below
Of bright gold, on silk bands enriched with stripes,
And so the knight rides with slippers on his feet
And all that he was wearing was indeed pure verdure
But the crossbars of his belt and the shining stones set
Resplendent here and there in his gleaming garments
All around him and his saddle, (in silk embroidery—
It would be too hard to tell half of the details
That were there in fine stitches, with birds and butterflies)
In a high green radiance with gold running through it.
The tassels of his horse's trappings and the handsome crupper,
The studs on the enameled bit and all the other metal,
And the stirrups that he stood in were of the same color,
And his saddle bow also and the rest of the fastenings,
It all kept glimmering and glinting with green stones.
The horse that he was riding resplendent with the same hue
          as all the rest.
     A green horse, hard to handle,
     A strong steed, huge and massive,

In brawden brydel quik—
To þe gome he watz ful gayn.

Wel gay watz þis gome gered in grene,
And þe here of his hed of his hors swete.                    180
Fayre fannand fax vmbefoldes his schulderes;
A much berd as a busk ouer his brest henges,
Þat wyth his hiȝlich here þat of his hed reches
Watz euesed al vmbetorne abof his elbowes,
Þat half his armes þer-vnder were halched in þe wyse        185
Of a kyngez capados þat closes his swyre;
Þe mane of þat mayn hors much to hit lyke,
Wel cresped and cemmed, wyth knottes ful mony
Folden in wyth fildore aboute þe fayre grene,
Ay a herle of þe here, an oþer of golde;                    190
Þe tayl and his toppyng twynnen of a sute,
And bounden boþe wyth a bande of a bryȝt grene,
Dubbed wyth ful dere stonez, as þe dok lasted,
Syþen þrawen wyth a þwong a þwarle knot alofte,
Þer mony bellez ful bryȝt of brende golde rungen.          195
Such a fole vpon folde, ne freke þat hym rydes,
Watz neuer sene in þat sale wyth syȝt er þat tyme,
              with yȝe.
        He loked as layt so lyȝt,
        So sayd al þat hym syȝe;                            200
        Hit semed as no mon myȝt
        Vnder his dynttez dryȝe.

Wheþer hade he no helme ne hawbergh nauþer,
Ne no pysan ne no plate þat pented to armes,
Ne no schafte ne no schelde to schwue ne to smyte,         205
Bot in his on honde he hade a holyn bobbe,

[ 14 ]

Tossing the embroidered bridle,
The right horse for that knight to have.

How splendid he looked, this knight in the green apparel,
And his horse's hair was as lovely as his own.
Fair waving locks tumbled around his shoulders,
A beard big as a bush flowing over his breast,
And the full length of the noble hair of his head
Had been cut in a circle above his elbows
So that his arms were half hidden under it
As by the tunic that covers a king's neck.
The mane of that mighty horse looked much like that,
Its curls well combed and caught into many knots
With gold cord wound around the bright green,
For every strand of hair another of gold.
His tail and his forelocks were enwound the same way,
And both were bound with a band of bright green
And precious stones adorning them to the tip of his tail,
Then laced up tightly in a twirled knot.
There many bright shining bells of fine gold were ringing.
No knight rides a horse like that anywhere on earth.
Never before had one been seen in that hall
       by anyone.
    Bright as lightning he shone, *very grand and*
    So they all said who saw him. *rich*
    It seemed that no man
    Could stand against him.

[Yet he wore no helmet and no chain mail either,] *didn't come to fight*
Nor any breastplate, nor brassarts on his arms,
He had no spear and no shield for thrusting and striking,
But in his hand he held a branch of holly

Þat is grattest in grene when greuez ar bare,
And an ax in his oþer, a hoge and vnmete,
A spetos sparþe to expoun in spelle, quoso my3t.
Þe lenkþe of an eln3erde þe large hede hade,          210
Þe grayn al of grene stele and of golde hewen,
Þe bit burnyst bry3t, with a brod egge
As wel schapen to schere as scharp rasores,
Þe stele of a stif staf þe sturne hit bi grypte,
Þat watz wounden wyth yrn to þe wandez ende,
And al bigrauen with grene in gracios werkes;          216
A lace lapped aboute, þat louked at þe hede,
And so after þe halme halched ful ofte,
Wyth tryed tasselez þerto tacched innoghe
On botounz of þe bry3t grene brayden ful ryche.          220
Þis haþel heldez hym in and þe halle entres,
Driuande to þe he3e dece, dut he no woþe,
Haylsed he neuer one, bot he3e he ouer loked.
Þe fyrst word þat he warp, 'Wher is', he sayd,
'Þe gouernour of þis gyng? Gladly I wolde          225
Se þat segg in sy3t, and with hymself speke
      raysoun.'
         To kny3tez he kest his y3e,
         And reled hym vp and doun;
         He stemmed, and con studie          230
         Quo walt þer most renoun.

Ther watz lokyng on lenþe þe lude to beholde,
For vch mon had meruayle quat hit mene my3t
Þat a haþel and a horse my3t such a hwe lach,
As growe grene as þe gres and grener hit semed,          235
Þen grene aumayl on golde glowande bry3ter.
Al studied þat þer stod, and stalked hym nerre

That is greenest of all when the groves are bare, green also for evergreen

And an ax in the other hand, huge and monstrous,

A fearsome battle-ax to find words to tell of.

The length of its head was at least a yard and a half,

The point all hammered out of green steel and gold,

The blade brightly burnished, with a broad edge,

Shaped for shearing as well as sharp razors.

The grim knight gripped the stout handle of the weapon.

It was wrapped with iron to the shaft's end

And all engraved with green in graceful designs.

A lace was wound around it, fastened at the head,

Twining in many turns around the handle

With a fringe of fine tassels attached to it,

Rich embroidery above buttons of bright green.

This knight rides straight ahead into the hall,

Making for the high dais, undaunted by anything,

With no greeting to anyone, but his eyes high above them.

The first sound from him: "Where," he asked, "is

The head of this gathering? I would be glad

To set eyes on that knight, and I have something

       to say to him."

      Over the knights he cast his eye

      Riding up and down,

      Stopping and looking hard to see

      Who might have most renown.


They went on staring at the knight for some time,

Everyone wondering what it might mean

For a man and a horse to acquire such a color,

As green as the grass grows, and greener still, it seemed,

The green enamel glowing brighter on the gold.

All of them standing there stared and crept closer to him

Wyth al þe wonder of þe worlde what he worch schulde.
For fele sellyez had þay sen, bot such neuer are;
Forþi for fantoum and fayry3e þe folk þere hit demed.                    240
Perfore to answare watz ar3e mony aþel freke,
And al stouned at his steuen and stonstil seten
In a swoghe sylence þur3 þe sale riche;
As al were slypped vpon slepe so slaked hor lotez
        in hy3e—                                                                    245
      I deme hit not al for doute,
      Bot sum for cortaysye—
      Bot let hym þat al schulde loute
      Cast vnto þat wy3e.

Penn Arþour bifore þe hi3 dece þat auenture byholdez,                    250
And rekenly hym reuerenced, for rad was he neuer,
And sayde, 'Wy3e, welcum iwys to þis place,
Pe hede of þis ostel Arthour I hat;
Li3t luflych adoun and lenge, I þe praye,
And quat-so þy wylle is we schal wyt after.'                             255
'Nay, as help me,' quoþ þe haþel, 'he þat on hy3e syttes,
To wone any quyle in þis won, hit watz not myn ernde;
Bot for þe los of þe, lede, is lyft vp so hy3e,
And þy bur3 and þy burnes best ar holden,
Stifest vnder stel-gere on stedes to ryde,                              260
Pe wy3test and þe worþyest of þe worldes kynde,
Preue for to play wyth in oþer pure laykez,
And here is kydde cortaysye, as I haf herd carp,
And þat hatz wayned me hider, iwyis, at þis tyme.
3e may be seker bi þis braunch þat I bere here                          265
Pat I passe as in pes, and no ply3t seche;
For had I founded in fere in fe3tyng wyse,

With all the wonder in the world, to see what he would do.
For they had seen many marvels but never any like this,
So they all thought it might be a phantom or trick of magic,
So that many of the noble knights were afraid to answer,
And all were struck by his voice and stayed stone still,
And there was a silence like death through the great hall.
Not a sound rose out of them, as though they had all
   fallen asleep.
    Not, I think, from fear only,
    But some waiting for
    Their King, out of courtesy,
    To let him answer.

Then Arthur, addressing this wonder before the high dais,
Greeted him courteously, for nothing ever frightened him,
And said, "Knight, you are welcome indeed in this place.
My name is Arthur. I am the head of this house.
I pray you to have the grace to dismount and stay with us
And whatever you want we shall learn later."
"No, as I hope for help," the knight said, "from Him who sits on high,
It was never my mission to stay long in this house.
But because your fame, sire, is so exalted
And your castles and your knights are said to be
The best and strongest who ride in armor on horses,
The bravest and most noble anywhere in the world,
Worthy to contend with for the pure play of it,
And I have heard of the famous chivalry of this place,
All of that, I may tell you, brought me here at this time.
You may be assured by this branch that I bear here
That I am passing through in peace and not looking for enemies,
For if I had set out intent upon fighting

I haue a hauberghe at home and a helme boþe,
A schelde and a scharp spere, schinande bry3t,
Ande oþer weppenes to welde, I wene wel, als;     270
Bot for I wolde no were, my wedez ar softer.
Bot if þou be so bold as alle burnez tellen,
Þou wyl grant me godly þe gomen þat I ask
        bi ry3t.'
      Arthour con onsware,     275
      And sayd, 'Sir cortays kny3t,
      If þou craue batayl bare,
      Here faylez þou not to fy3t.'

'Nay, frayst I no fy3t, in fayth I þe telle,
Hit arn aboute on þis bench bot berdlez chylder.     280
If I were hasped in armes on a he3e stede,
Here is no mon me to mach, for my3tez so wayke.
Forþy I craue in þis court a Crystemas gomen,
For hit is 3ol and Nwe 3er, and here ar 3ep mony:
If any so hardy in þis hous holdez hymseluen,     285
Be so bolde in his blod, brayn in hys hede,
Þat dar stifly strike a strok for an oþer,
I schal gif hym of my gyft þys giserne ryche,
Þis ax, þat is heué innogh, to hondele as hym lykes,
And I schal bide þe fyrst bur as bare as I sitte.
If any freke be so felle to fonde þat I telle,     291
Lepe ly3tly me to, and lach þis weppen,
I quit-clayme hit for euer, kepe hit as his auen,
And I schal stonde hym a strok, stif on þis flet,
Ellez þou wyl di3t me þe dom to dele hym an oþer     295
        barlay,
      And 3et gif hym respite,
      A twelmonyth and a day;

I have chain mail at home, and helmet too,
A shield and a sharp spear shining brightly,  *flexing*
And other weapons to wield also, to be sure.
But since I did not come for fighting, my clothes are softer.
But if you are as bold as knights everywhere say you are,
You will be so good as to grant me the request that I
        have the right to ask."
      Arthur gave the knight
      This answer: "Courteous sir,
      Whatever sport or fight
      You came for, you will find here."


"No, I tell you in good faith, it is not a fight I have come for.
These are nothing but beardless boys around this bench.
If I were buckled in armor on a big horse,  *owned...*
There is no man here strong enough to be worth riding against.
And so in this court I call for a Christmas game,
Since it is Yuletide and the New Year and all these brave men are here:
If anyone in this house thinks he has the courage
And is so bold in his blood and wild in his way of thinking
That he dares to exchange one heavy blow for another,
I shall make him a gift of this great battle-ax,
And a heavy one it is, this ax, to handle as he pleases,
And I shall await the first blow without armor, just as I sit here.
If any knight is brave enough to test my word,
Run up to me right now and take hold of this weapon.
I give it up for good, he can keep it as his own,
And I shall take a stroke from him on this floor, without flinching.
Then you must grant me the right to give him one in return
      without resisting,  *if someone hits me they*
      But for that one he  *get the axe but I*
      May wait a year and a day.  *get to hit him back*
                 *in a year*

[ 21 ]

Now hyȝe, and let se tite
Dar any herinne oȝt say.'                                300

If he hem stowned vpon fyrst, stiller were þanne
Alle þe heredmen in halle, þe hyȝ and þe loȝe.
Þe renk on his rouncé hym ruched in his sadel,
And runischly his rede yȝen he reled aboute,
Bende his bresed broȝez, blycande grene,              305
Wayued his berde for to wayte quo-so wolde ryse.
When non wolde kepe hym with carp he coȝed ful hyȝe,
Ande rimed hym ful richely, and ryȝt hym to speke:
'What, is þis Arþures hous,' quoþ þe haþel þenne,
'Þat al þe rous rennes of þurȝ ryalmes so mony?       310
Where is now your sourquydrye and your conquestes,
Your gryndellayk and your greme, and your grete wordes?
Now is þe reuel and þe renoun of þe Rounde Table
Ouerwalt wyth a worde of on wyȝes speche,
For al dares for drede withoute dynt schewed!'        315
Wyth þis he laȝes so loude þat þe lorde greued;
Þe blod schot for scham into his schyre face
            and lere;
        He wex as wroth as wynde,
        So did alle þat þer were.                     320
        Þe kyng as kene bi kynde
        Þen stod þat stif mon nere,

Ande sayde, 'Haþel, by heuen, þyn askyng is nys,
And as þou foly hatz frayst, fynde þe behoues.
I know no gome þat is gast of þy grete wordes;        325
Gif me now þy geserne, vpon Godez halue,
And I schal bayþen þy bone þat þou boden habbes.'
Lyȝtly lepez he hym to, and laȝt at his honde.

[ 22 ]

Now let me see
What anyone here has to say."

If he had stunned them at first, then they were even more still,
All the courtiers in the hall, the high and the low.
The knight on his horse turned in his saddle,
And wildly he flashed his red eyes around,
Arched his bristling bright-green eyebrows,
And waved his beard, waiting to see who would stand up.
When no one would answer him, he gave a loud cough
And stretched as a lord might, and made ready to speak.
"Well, is this Arthur's house," the knight said then,
"That all the talk runs on through so many kingdoms?
Where is your haughtiness now, where are your triumphs,
Your belligerence and your wrath and your big words?
Now the revel and the renown of the Round Table
Are overturned by a word of one man alone,
All cowering in dread before a blow has been struck."
With this he roars with such laughter that the lord was angry.
Shame shot the blood into his white face
                    and his cheeks.
          Like the wind was his anger.
          It swept through everyone.
          The King, bold by nature,
          Went up to that huge man

And said, "Knight, by heaven, your request is senseless.
What you ask is such madness you deserve to have it granted.
No knight I know is afraid of your great words.
Give me your ax now, in the name of God,
And I shall grant the boon that you have requested."
He strides toward him and grasps him by the hand.

Þen feersly þat oþer freke vpon fote ly3tis.
Now hatz Arthure his axe, and þe halme grypez,            330
And sturnely sturez hit aboute, þat stryke wyth hit þo3t.
Þe stif mon hym bifore stod vpon hy3t,
Herre þen ani in þe hous by þe hede and more.
Wyth sturne schere þer he stod he stroked his berde,
And wyth a countenaunce dry3e he dro3 doun his cote,      335
No more mate ne dismayd for hys mayn dintez
Þen any burne vpon bench hade bro3t hym to drynk
      of wyne.
        Gawan, þat sate bi þe quene,
        To þe kyng he can enclyne:                340
        'I beseche now with sa3ez sene
        Þis melly mot be myne.

'Wolde 3e, worþilych lorde,' quoþ Wawan to þe kyng,
'Bid me bo3e fro þis benche, and stonde by yow þere,
Þat I wythoute vylanye my3t voyde þis table,             345
And þat my legge lady lyked not ille,
I wolde com to your counseyl bifore your cort ryche.
For me þink hit not semly, as hit is soþ knawen,
Þer such an askyng is heuened so hy3e in your sale,
Þa3 3e 3ourself be talenttyf, to take hit to yourseluen,  350
Whil mony so bolde yow aboute vpon bench sytten,
Þat vnder heuen I hope non ha3erer of wylle,
Ne better bodyes on bent þer baret is rered.
I am þe wakkest, I wot, and of wyt feblest,
And lest lur of my lyf, quo laytes þe soþe—              355
Bot for as much as 3e ar myn em I am only to prayse,
No bounté bot your blod I in my bodé knowe;
And syþen þis note is so nys þat no3t hit yow falles,

Then proudly that other knight sets foot on the ground.
Now Arthur has his ax, gripping the handle,
And grimly swings it around, preparing to strike with it.
The bold man stood towering before him,
Taller than any in the house by a head and more.
With a grim look on his face he stood there and stroked his beard,
[And with unmoved expression he pulled down his tunic, *nothing*
No more daunted nor dismayed before that great stroke *happens*
Than he would have been if a knight had brought him, at table,)
      a drink of wine.

        Gawain, sitting next to the Queen,
        Bowed to the King then:
        "I will keep my words plain.
        I ask for this battle to be mine."


"If you please, glorious lord," Gawain said to the King,
"I will turn from this table and stand by you there,
If I may do that without discourtesy,
And without displeasing my liege lady,
I would come to your counsel before your great court,
For I think it not proper, according to our customs,
For such a request to be put so high in your hall
That you feel moved to reply to it yourself
When so many of the bravest are about you on the bench.
There are no better warriors, I believe, under heaven,
No better bodies on earth, when the battle begins.
I am the weakest, I know, and the least wise, *everything good*
And cling least to my life, if anyone wants the truth, *dude :(*
But as you are my uncle whom I live to praise
And your blood is the sole virtue in my body, *:s*
And since this affair is so foolish, it does not befit you.

And I haue frayned hit at yow fyrst, foldez hit to me;
And if I carp not comlyly, let alle þis cort rych                360
       bout blame.'
    Ryche togeder con roun,
    And syþen þay redden alle same
    To ryd þe kyng wyth croun,
    And gif Gawan þe game.                               365

Þen comaunded þe kyng þe knyȝt for to ryse;
And he ful radly vpros, and ruchched hym fayre,
Kneled doun bifore þe kyng, and cachez þat weppen;
And he luflyly hit hym laft, and lyfte vp his honde,
And gef hym Goddez blessyng, and gladly hym biddes           370
Þat his hert and his honde schulde hardi be boþe.
'Kepe þe, cosyn,' quoþ þe kyng, 'þat þou on kyrf sette,
And if þou redez hym ryȝt, redly I trowe
Þat þou schal byden þe bur þat he schal bede after.'
Gawan gotz to þe gome with giserne in honde,                 375
And he baldly hym bydez, he bayst neuer þe helder.
Þen carppez to Sir Gawan þe knyȝt in þe grene,
'Refourme we oure forwardes, er we fyrre passe.
Fyrst I eþe þe, haþel, how þat þou hattes
Þat þou me telle truly, as I tryst may.'                     380
'In god fayth,' quoþ þe goode knyȝt, 'Gawan I hatte,
Þat bede þe þis buffet, quat-so bifallez after,
And at þis tyme twelmonyth take at þe an oþer
Wyth what weppen so þou wylt, and wyth no wyȝ ellez
       on lyue.'                                385
    Þat oþer onswarez agayn,
    'Sir Gawan, so mot I þryue
    As I am ferly fayn
    Þis dint þat þou schal dryue.

I have asked this of you first, and beg you to grant it,
And if my request is improper, I ask this great court
        not to blame me."
     All the court began whispering
     And all thought the same:
     Relieve the crowned King
     And let Gawain have the game.

Then the King commanded the knight to rise
And he leapt to his feet and turned gracefully,
Knelt before the King and took hold of the weapon.
The King let go of it and lifted his hand,
Gave him God's blessing and was glad to hope
That his heart and his hand would both be hardy.
"Take care, cousin," the King said, "how you make your cut,
And if you strike as you should, it seems certain to me
You will endure the blow he gives you in return."
Gawain goes to the knight with ax in hand
And the knight waits for him boldly, utterly undaunted.
Then the knight in green said to Sir Gawain,
"Let us repeat our agreement before we go further.
First, knight, I inquire of you what your name is,
And you tell me that truthfully, as I trust you will."
"In good faith," the good knight said, "my name is Gawain,
Who offer you this blow, whatever it leads to,
And twelve months from now I will take from you another
With what weapon you will, and not otherwise
        in the world."
     That other knight answers then,
     "I welcome this stroke,
     Upon my life, Gawain,
     That you are about to make."

'Bigog,' quoþ þe grene knyȝt, 'Sir Gawan, me lykes       390
Þat I schal fange at þy fust þat I haf frayst here.
And þou hatz redily rehersed, bi resoun ful trwe,
Clanly al þe couenaunt þat I þe kynge asked,
Saf þat þou schal siker me, segge, bi þi trawþe,
Þat þou schal seche me þiself, where-so þou hopes     395
I may be funde vpon folde, and foch þe such wages
As þou deles me to-day bifore þis douþe ryche.'
'Where schulde I wale þe,' quoþ Gauan, 'where is þy place?
I wot neuer where þou wonyes, bi hym þat me wroȝt,
Ne I know not þe, knyȝt, þy cort ne þi name.      400
Bot teche me truly þerot, and telle me how þou hattes,
And I schal ware alle my wyt to wynne me þeder,
And þat I swere þe for soþe, and by my seker traweþ.'
'Þat is innogh in Nwe Ȝer, hit nedes no more',
Quoþ þe gome in þe grene to Gawan þe hende;     405
'Ȝif I þe telle trwly, quen I þe tape haue
And þou me smoþely hatz smyten, smartly I þe teche
Of my hous and my home and myn owen nome,
Þen may þou frayst my fare and forwardez holde;
And if I spende no speche, þenne spedez þou þe better,   410
For þou may leng in þy londe and layt no fyrre—
       bot slokes!
         Ta now þy grymme tole to þe,
         And let se how þou cnokez.'
         'Gladly, sir, for soþe',     415
         Quoþ Gawan; his ax he strokes.


The grene knyȝt vpon grounde grayþely hym dresses,
A littel lut with þe hede, þe lere he discouerez,
His longe louelych lokkez he layd ouer his croun,
Let the naked nec to þe note schewe.      420

"By God," the Green Knight said, "I am glad
That I shall have from your hand what I asked for here,
And that you have repeated fully, in your own words,
The whole of the covenant I asked of the King:
Only now you must swear to me, upon your word,
That you will expect, for yourself, wherever you manage
To find me on earth, to be repaid in kind
For what you accord me today before this high company."
"Where shall I find you?" Gawain asked. "Where is your place?
I do not know where you live, by him that made me,
Nor do I know you, knight, nor your house nor your name.
Only tell me the truth about that, and what your name is,
And I shall use all my wits to make my way there,
And I swear to this on my word as a knight."
"That is enough for this New Year, no more need be said,"
The Green Knight said to the courteous Gawain.
"The truth is that when I have taken the blow,
And you have struck me soundly, I will tell you then
About my house and my home and my own name.
Then you will find out about me and how to keep our agreement,
And if I say nothing, so much the better for you,
And you may live long in your land and not have to look further—
            but enough!
        Pick up your grim tool now
        And let us see how you handle it."
        "Gladly, sir, I promise you,"
        Gawain said, stroking it.


The Green Knight takes his stand without lingering
And bends his head a little to show the skin.
He laid his long graceful locks across his crown,
Leaving the naked neck bare and ready.

Gauan gripped to his ax, and gederes hit on hy3t,
Þe kay fot on þe folde he before sette,
Let hit doun ly3tly ly3t on þe naked,
Þat þe scharp of þe schalk schyndered þe bones,
And schrank pur3 þe schyire grece, and schade hit in twynne,       425
Þat þe bit of þe broun stel bot on þe grounde.
Þe fayre hede fro þe halce hit to þe erþe,
Þat fele hit foyned wyth her fete, þere hit forth roled;
Þe blod brayd fro þe body, þat blykked on þe grene;
And nawþer faltered ne fel þe freke neuer þe helder,       430
Bot styþly he start forth vpon styf schonkes,
And runyschly he ra3t out, þere as renkkez stoden,
La3t to his lufly hed, and lyft hit vp sone;
And syþen bo3ez to his blonk, þe brydel he cachchez,
Steppez into stelbawe and strydez alofte,       435
And his hede by þe here in his honde haldez;
And as sadly þe segge hym in his sadel sette
As non vnhap had hym ayled, þa3 hedlez he were
          in stedde.
      He brayde his bulk aboute,       440
      Þat vgly bodi þat bledde;
      Moni on of hym had doute,
      Bi þat his resounz were redde.


For þe hede in his honde he haldez vp euen,
Toward þe derrest on þe dece he dressez þe face,       445
And hit lyfte vp þe y3e-lyddez and loked ful brode,
And meled þus much with his muthe, as 3e may now here:
'Loke, Gawan, þou be grayþe to go as þou hettez,
And layte as lelly til þou me, lude, fynde,
As þou hatz hette in þis halle, herande þise kny3tes;       450
To þe grene chapel þou chose, I charge þe, to fotte

Gawain gripped his ax and heaved it up high.
He set his left foot on the ground in front of him
And brought the blade down suddenly onto the bare skin
So that the sharp edge sundered the man's bones
And sank through the white flesh and sliced it in two

*A trial*

Until the bright steel of the bit sank into the ground.
The handsome head fell from the neck to the earth

*ok... he killed a dude*

And rolled out among their feet so that they kicked it.)
The blood gushed from the body, glittering over the green,
And the knight never staggered or fell, for all that,
But he stepped forth as strong as ever, on unshaken legs,
And reached in roughly among the knights
To snatch up his lovely head and at once lift it high.
And then he turns to his horse and takes hold of the bridle,
Steps into the stirrup and swings himself up,
Holding his head in his hand by the hair,

*very metal.*

And settles into the saddle as firmly as ever
With no trouble at all, though he sits there
       headless.
       All around him the blood sprayed
       As his gruesome body bled.
       Many of them were afraid
       When they heard what he said.


For he holds the head up high in his hand,
Turning the face toward the noblest on the platform,
And it raised its eyelids and opened its eyes wide
And said this much with its mouth, which you may hear now:
"Remember, Gawain, to get ready for what you agreed to,
And search carefully, knight, until you find me
As you have sworn to do in this hall where these knights heard you.
I charge you to make your way to the Green Chapel

Such a dunt as þou hatz dalt—disserued þou habbez
To be ȝederly ȝolden on Nw Ȝeres morn.
Þe knyȝt of þe grene chapel men knowen me mony;
Forþi me for to fynde if þou fraystez, faylez þou neuer.        455
Þerfore com, oþer recreaunt be calde þe behoues.'
With a runisch rout þe raynez he tornez,
Halled out at þe hal dor, his hed in his hande,
Þat þe fyr of þe flynt flaȝe fro fole houes.
To quat kyth he becom knwe non þere,                           460
Neuer more þen þay wyste from queþen he watz wonnen.
          What þenne?
            Þe kyng and Gawen þare
            At þat grene þay laȝe and grenne,
            Ȝet breued watz hit ful bare                       465
            A meruayl among þo menne.


Þaȝ Arþer þe hende kyng at hert hade wonder,
He let no semblaunt be sene, bot sayde ful hyȝe
To þe comlych quene wyth cortays speche,
'Dere dame, to-day demay yow neuer;                            470
Wel bycommes such craft vpon Cristmasse,
Laykyng of enterludez, to laȝe and to syng,
Among þise kynde caroles of knyȝtez and ladyez.
Neuer þe lece to my mete I may me wel dres,
For I haf sen a selly, I may not forsake.'                     475
He glent vpon Sir Gawen, and gaynly he sayde,
'Now sir, heng vp þyn ax, þat hatz innogh hewen';
And hit watz don abof þe dece on doser to henge,
Þer alle men for meruayl myȝt on hit loke,
And bi trwe tytel þerof to telle þe wonder.                    480
Þenne þay boȝed to a borde þise burnes togeder,

To receive a stroke like the one you have given—you have earned it—
To be repaid promptly on New Year's morning.
Many men know me as the Knight of the Green Chapel,
So if you ask, you cannot fail to find me.
Come then, or you will rightly be called a coward."
With a terrible roar he turns the reins,
Rides out through the hall door, his head in his hand,
So that the flint flashes fire from his horse's hooves.
No one there knew what land he was going to
Any more than they knew where he had come from.
            What then?
        Gawain and the King smile
        And laugh about that green man.
        All agreed that he was marvel
        Enough for anyone.

In his heart Arthur, that noble king, was stunned.
He allowed no sign of it to show but said aloud,
Gently, courteously, to the beautiful Queen,
"Beloved lady, do not be troubled by what happened today.
Things of this kind can occur at Christmastime,   *CAN THEY??*
With the performing of plays, the laughing and singing,
And carols and courtly dances of knights and ladies.
Just the same, I may well turn to my meal now,
For I have seen a wonder, I cannot deny it."
He glanced at Sir Gawain and, making light of it, said,
"Now, sir, hang up your ax, which has hewn enough,"
And it was done, above the dais, attached to a tapestry,
Where everyone might stare at it as a marvel
And try to find words for the wonder of it.
Then all those knights turned together to the table,

Þe kyng and þe gode kny3t, and kene men hem serued
Of alle dayntyez double, as derrest my3t falle;
Wyth alle maner of mete and mynstralcie boþe,
Wyth wele walt þay þat day, til worþed an ende          485
       in londe.
         Now þenk wel, Sir Gawan,
         For woþe þat þou ne wonde
         Þis auenture for to frayn
         Þat þou hatz tan on honde.          490

The King, and the good knight, and bold men served them
Double of all the fine dishes, whatever was most delicious.
There was all manner of food and also of minstrelsy.
They spent that day in pleasures until it came to an end
        on the earth.
        Now take thought, Sir Gawain,
        Of the danger before you,
        The risk to be run,
        Which you have taken upon you.

*address him!!*

# II

This hanselle hatz Arthur of auenturus on fyrst
In ȝonge ȝer, for he ȝerned ȝelpyng to here.
Thaȝ hym wordez were wane when þay to sete wenten,
Now ar þay stoken of sturne werk, stafful her hond.
Gawan watz glad to begynne þose gomnez in halle,                    495
Bot þaȝ þe ende be heuy haf ȝe no wonder;
For þaȝ men ben mery in mynde quen þay han mayn drynk,
A ȝere ȝernes ful ȝerne, and ȝeldez neuer lyke,
Þe forme to þe fynisment foldez ful selden.
Forþi þis ȝol ouerȝede, and þe ȝere after,                         500
And vche sesoun serlepes sued after oþer:
After Crystenmasse com þe crabbed lentoun,
Þat fraystez flesch wyth þe fysche and fode more symple;
Bot þenne þe weder of þe worlde wyth wynter hit þrepez,
Colde clengez adoun, cloudez vplyften,                             505
Schyre schedez þe rayn in schowrez ful warme,
Fallez vpon fayre flat, flowrez þere schewen,
Boþe groundez and þe greuez grene ar her wedez,
Bryddez busken to bylde, and bremlych syngen
For solace of þe softe somer þat sues þerafter                     510
  bi bonk;
   And blossumez bolne to blowe
   Bi rawez rych and ronk,
   Þen notez noble innoȝe
   Ar herde in wod so wlonk.

# II

This wonder came as a gift to Arthur in the first
Youth of the year, for he longed to hear of some bold adventure.
Though their words were few when they first sat to table,
Soon they had more to say than they had words for.
Gawain was glad to begin those games in the hall,
But if the mood grew heavy at last it was no wonder,
For though after strong drink men may be merry in their minds,
A year soon runs its length and never returns the same,
And the end seldom seems to belong to the beginning.
So this Christmas was over then, and the last of the year followed it,
And the seasons went by in turn one after the other.
After Christmas came crabbèd Lent
That chastises the flesh with fish and plainer food.
But then the weather of the world makes war on winter,
Cold cringes downward, clouds lift,
The shining rain comes down in warm showers,
Falls on the fair meadow, flowers appear there,
Both the open land and the groves are in green garments,
Birds hurry to build, and they sing gloriously
With the joy of the soft summer that arrives
        on all the hills,
     And blossoms are opening
     In thick hedgerows, and then the noblest
     Of all songs ring
     Through the lovely forest.

After þe sesoun of somer wyth þe soft wyndez      516
Quen Zeferus syflez hymself on sedez and erbez,
Wela wynne is þe wort þat waxes þeroute,
When þe donkande dewe dropez of þe leuez,
To bide a blysful blusch of þe bry3t sunne.      520
Bot þen hy3es heruest, and hardenes hym sone,
Warnez hym for þe wynter to wax ful rype;
He dryues wyth dro3t þe dust for to ryse,
Fro þe face of þe folde to fly3e ful hy3e;
Wroþe wynde of þe welkyn wrastelez with þe sunne,      525
Þe leuez lancen fro þe lynde and ly3ten on þe grounde,
And al grayes þe gres þat grene watz ere;
Þenne al rypez and rotez þat ros vpon fyrst,
And þus 3irnez þe 3ere in 3isterdayez mony,
And wynter wyndez a3ayn, as þe worlde askez,      530
        no fage,
     Til Me3elmas mone
     Watz cumen wyth wynter wage;
     Þen þenkkez Gawan ful sone
     Of his anious uyage.      535

3et quyl Al-hal-day with Arþer he lenges;
And he made a fare on þat fest for þe frekez sake,
With much reuel and ryche of þe Rounde Table.
Kny3tez ful cortays and comlych ladies
Al for luf of þat lede in longynge þay were,      540
Bot neuer þe lece ne þe later þay neuened bot merþe:
Mony ioylez for þat ientyle iapez þer maden.
For after mete with mournyng he melez to his eme,
And spekez of his passage, and pertly he sayde,
'Now, lege lorde of my lyf, leue I yow ask;      545
3e knowe þe cost of þis cace, kepe I no more

Then comes the season of summer with the soft winds,
When Zephyrus breathes gently on the seeds and grasses.
Happy is the green leaf that grows out of that time
When the wet of the dew drips from the leaves
Before the blissful radiance of the bright sun.
But then comes harvest time to hearten them,
Warning them to ripen well before winter.
It brings drought until the dust rises,
Flying up high off the face of the field,
A fierce wind wrestles with the sun in the heavens,
The leaves fly from the lime tree and light on the ground,
And the grass is all withered that before was green. *knight...*
Then all that was growing at first ripens and decays,
And thus in many yesterdays the year passes
And winter comes back again as the world would have it,
             in the way of things.
        Until the Michaelmas moon
        When first the days feel wintry
        And Gawain is reminded then
        Of his dread journey.


Still he stays until All Saints' Day with Arthur
And kept that feast with them for the sake of the knights,
With revelry and high spirits at the Round Table.
Noble knights and beautiful ladies
Were all grieving out of love for that knight,
But nevertheless they gave words to nothing but mirth.
Many made jests who were joyless because of that gentle knight.
And after the meal he speaks sadly to his uncle
About his journey, and in plain words he said,
"Now, liege lord of my life, I must ask to take leave of you.
You know the terms of this promise. I do not care

To telle yow tenez þerof, neuer bot trifel;
Bot I am boun to þe bur barely to-morne
To sech þe gome of þe grene, as God wyl me wysse.'
Þenne þe best of þe burȝ boȝed togeder,                    550
Aywan, and Errik, and oþer ful mony,
Sir Doddinaual de Sauage, þe duk of Clarence,
Launcelot, and Lyonel, and Lucan þe gode,
Sir Boos, and Sir Byduer, big men boþe,
And mony oþer menskful, with Mador de la Port.            555
Alle þis compayny of court com þe kyng nerre
For to counseyl þe knyȝt, with care at her hert.
Þere watz much derue doel driuen in þe sale
Þat so worthé as Wawan schulde wende on þat ernde,
To dryȝe a delful dynt, and dele no more                  560
          wyth bronde.
          Þe knyȝt mad ay god chere,
          And sayde, 'Quat schuld I wonde?
          Of destinés derf and dere
          What may mon do bot fonde?'                      565

He dowellez þer al þat day, and dressez on þe morn,
Askez erly hys armez, and alle were þay broȝt.
Fyrst a tulé tapit tyȝt ouer þe flet,
And miche watz þe gyld gere þat glent þeralofte;
Þe stif mon steppez þeron, and þe stel hondelez,          570
Dubbed in a dublet of a dere tars,
And syþen a crafty capados, closed aloft,
Þat wyth a bryȝt blaunner was bounden withinne.
Þenne set þay þe sabatounz vpon þe segge fotez,
His legez lapped in stel with luflych greuez,             575
With polaynez piched þerto, policed ful clene,
Aboute his knez knaged wyth knotez of golde;

To mention the trouble of it, not a word about that.
But I am bound to set out for that stroke tomorrow without fail,
To search for the Green Knight, as God may guide me."
Then the best of the knights gathered around:
Ywain and Eric and many others,
Sir Doddinaval de Savage, the Duke of Clarence,
Lancelot and Lionel, and the good Lucan,
Sir Bors and Sir Bedivere, big men both of them,
And many other noble knights, with Mador of the Gate.
All this company of the court crowded close to the King
To counsel the knight, out of the care in their hearts.
There was a great sharp grief passing through the hall
At so noble a one as Gawain going on that errand
To suffer a terrible blow and handle the sword

        no more.
      Still, the knight spoke cheerfully,
      Saying, "What should trouble me?
      In the face of harsh destiny
      What can a man do but try?"

*[handwritten margin note: sort of change of mentality since start]*

He stays there all that day and makes ready the next morning,
Calls early for his arms and they were all brought to him.
First a red silk tapestry was spread on the floor
With a great mound of gilded armor gleaming on top of it.
The brave knight steps onto it and picks up the steel,
Dons a doublet of rich Tarsian silk,
Then a leather tunic cleverly cut to close at the top,
And all the inside lined with pure white fur.
Then they set the broad steel shoes on the knight's feet,
Elegant greaves encased his legs with steel
With knee pieces buckled to them, burnished brightly
And fastened with gold knots around his knees.

*[handwritten margin note: Stanza 25]*

Queme quyssewes þen, þat coyntlych closed
His thik þrawen þyȝez, with þwonges to tachched;
And syþen þe brawden bryné of bryȝt stel ryngez          580
Vmbeweued þat wyȝ vpon wlonk stuffe,
And wel bornyst brace vpon his boþe armes,
With gode cowters and gay, and glouez of plate,
And alle þe godlych gere þat hym gayn schulde
              þat tyde;          585
      Wyth ryche cote-armure,
      His gold sporez spend with pryde,
      Gurde wyth a bront ful sure
      With silk sayn vmbe his syde.

When he watz hasped in armes, his harnays watz ryche:
Þe lest lachet oþer loupe lemed of golde.          591
So harnayst as he watz he herknez his masse,
Offred and honoured at þe heȝe auter.
Syþen he comez to þe kyng and to his cort-ferez,
Lachez lufly his leue at lordez and ladyez;          595
And þay hym kyst and conueyed, bikende hym to Kryst.
Bi þat watz Gryngolet grayth, and gurde with a sadel
Þat glemed ful gayly with mony golde frenges,
Ayquere naylet ful nwe, for þat note ryched;
Þe brydel barred aboute, with bryȝt golde bounden;          600
Þe apparayl of þe payttrure and of þe proude skyrtez,
Þe cropore and þe couertor, acorded wyth þe arsounez;
And al watz rayled on red ryche golde naylez,
Þat al glytered and glent as glem of þe sunne.
Þenne hentes he þe helme, and hastily hit kysses,          605
Þat watz stapled stifly, and stoffed wythinne.
Hit watz hyȝe on his hede, hasped bihynde,

Then graceful thigh pieces, completely covering
His thick-muscled thighs, were tied on with thongs,
And then the linked mail shirt of bright steel rings
All embedded in a noble fabric,
And well-burnished pieces on both of his arms,
With good, graceful elbow plates and gauntlets of silver,
And all the fine gear that was to help him,
      whatever might happen,
    With splendid coat armor,      *stirred up!!*
    Gold spurs fastened proudly on him,
    A sword of which he was sure
    Slung on a silk belt around him.


When he was dressed in his armor his garments were a glory.
The least latchet of its fastenings glittered with gold.
Then, armored as he was, he went to hear Mass
Offered and celebrated at the high altar.
After that he comes to the King and to his companions,
Takes his leave formally of lords and ladies,
And they kissed him and walked with him and commended him to Christ.
By then Gryngolet was ready, girt with a saddle
Glittering merrily with many gold fringes
And new studs everywhere, set for that journey.
The bridle with stripes around it bound with bright gold,
And the ornaments of the breast trappings and of the proud caparison,
The crupper and the coverlet, were the color of the saddle bow,
And all were set on a <u>red</u> ground with bright gold nails  *seems to be*
That flashed and glinted like the gleam of the sun.  *red in contrast*
Then he takes up the helmet and quickly kisses it.  *to knight?*
It was stoutly stapled and was padded inside.
It stood high on his head, fastened behind him,

Wyth a ly3tly vrysoun ouer þe auentayle,
Enbrawden and bounden wyth þe best gemmez
On brode sylkyn borde, and bryddez on semez,        610
As papiayez paynted peruyng bitwene,
Tortors and trulofez entayled so þyk
As mony burde þeraboute had ben seuen wynter
       in toune.
        Þe cercle watz more o prys        615
        Þat vmbeclypped hys croun,
        Of diamauntez a deuys
        Þat boþe were bry3t and broun.

Then þay schewed hym þe schelde, þat was of schyr goulez
Wyth þe pentangel depaynt of pure golde hwez.        620
He braydez hit by þe bauderyk, aboute þe hals kestes,
Þat bisemed þe segge semlyly fayre.
And quy þe pentangel apendez to þat prynce noble
I am in tent yow to telle, þof tary hyt me schulde:
Hit is a syngne þat Salamon set sumquyle        625
In bytoknyng of trawþe, bi tytle þat hit habbez,
For hit is a figure þat haldez fyue poyntez,
And vche lyne vmbelappez and loukez in oþer,
And ayquere hit is endelez; and Englych hit callen
Oueral, as I here, þe endeles knot.        630
Forþy hit acordez to þis kny3t and to his cler armez,
For ay faythful in fyue and sere fyue syþez
Gawan watz for gode knawen, and as golde pured,
Voyded of vche vylany, wyth vertuez ennourned
       in mote;        635
        Forþy þe pentangel nwe
        He ber in schelde and cote,

And above the visor there was a bright scarf
Embroidered and adorned with the finest of gems
On a broad silk border, and <u>birds</u> along the seams,    *the symbolism...*
Even parrots painted preening among them,
Turtle doves and true-love knots sewn there so densely,
Many women must have been working on it, there at court,
        for seven winters.
      The circlet was still more precious
      Around his crown:
      As many diamonds as you please,
      And brightly they shone.

Then they showed him the shield that was bright <u>red</u>
With the pentangle painted on it in pure gold.
He took it by the baldric and slung it around his neck,
And it appeared to be perfectly suited to him.
And why the pentangle was appropriate to that noble prince
I mean to tell you, though it delay me.
It is a sign that Solomon once established
As a <u>symbol of truth, which is what it stands for,</u>
For it is a figure that has five points,
And each line overlaps and locks into another,
And everywhere it is endless, and the English, whenever
They speak of it, <u>call it the endless knot,</u> as I do here.
And so it suits this knight and his bright heraldry,
For he was faithful in five things always, and in five ways.
Gawain was known as a good knight and as gold purified,
Clear of every crudeness, graced and protected
      by virtues.
      So on shield and coat armor
      He bore the new pentangle

As tulk of tale most trwe
And gentylest kny3t of lote.

Fyrst he watz funden fautlez in his fyue wyttez,                640
And efte fayled neuer þe freke in his fyue fyngres,
And alle his afyaunce vpon folde watz in þe fyue woundez
Þat Cryst ka3t on þe croys, as þe crede tellez;
And quere-so-euer þys mon in melly watz stad,
His þro þo3t watz in þat, þur3 alle oþer þyngez,               645
Þat alle his forsnes he feng at þe fyue joyez
Þat þe hende heuen-quene had of hir chylde;
At þis cause þe kny3t comlyche hade
In þe inore half of his schelde hir ymage depaynted,
Þat quen he blusched þerto his belde neuer payred.            650
Þe fyft fyue þat I finde þat þe frek vsed
Watz fraunchyse and fela3schyp forbe al þyng,
His clannes and his cortaysye croked were neuer,
And pité, þat passez alle poyntez, þyse pure fyue
Were harder happed on þat haþel þen on any oþer.             655
Now alle þese fyue syþez, for soþe, were fetled on þis kny3t,
And vchone halched in oþer, þat non ende hade,
And fyched vpon fyue poyntez, þat fayld neuer,
Ne samned neuer in no syde, ne sundred nouþer,
Withouten ende at any noke I oquere fynde,                    660
Whereeuer þe gomen bygan, or glod to an ende.
Þerfore on his schene schelde schapen watz þe knot
Ryally wyth red golde vpon rede gowlez,
Þat is þe pure pentaungel wyth þe peple called
      with lore.                                    665
    Now grayþed is Gawan gay,
    And la3t his launce ry3t þore,

That meant no one's speech could be truer,
No one's word more noble.

First he was found faultless in all his five senses,
And second, the knight's five fingers never failed him,
And all his faith upon earth was in the five wounds
Christ received on the cross, as the creed tells us,
And wherever this man found himself in the fighting,
His whole thought held to those through everything else,
And then all his courage came from the five joys
That the high Queen of Heaven had from her Child.
For this reason the knight had her portrait
Painted on the inside of his shield,
So that when his glance fell on it his heart never faltered.
The fifth five that the knight practiced, I find,
Were generosity, and fellowship especially,
Purity of heart and courtesy were never wanting in him,
And pity, that surpasses all the other points—these pure five
Were more closely bound to that knight than to any other.
And the five forms of them, in fact, were arrayed in him,
Each one braiding into another so that there was no end,
Running among the five points that were never lost,
That never met on any side nor were ever parted,
Without end anywhere at any angle, as I find,
Wherever the game began or ran toward an end.
Therefore the knot was emblazoned on his bright shield,
Royally in red gold on a red ground,
The design which the learned refer to as the pure
       pentangle.
      Now Gawain is resplendent and ready.
      Last he picked up his own spear

And gef hem alle goud day,
He wende for euermore.

He sperred þe sted with þe spurez and sprong on his way,    670
So stif þat þe ston-fyr stroke out þerafter.
Al þat seȝ þat semly syked in hert,
And sayde soþly al same segges til oþer,
Carande for þat comly: 'Bi Kryst, hit is scaþe
Þat þou, leude, schal be lost, þat art of lyf noble!    675
To fynde hys fere vpon folde, in fayth, is not eþe.
Warloker to haf wroȝt had more wyt bene,
And haf dyȝt ȝonder dere a duk to haue worþed;
A lowande leder of ledez in londe hym wel semez,
And so had better haf ben þen britned to noȝt,    680
Hadet wyth an aluisch mon, for angardez pryde.
Who knew euer any kyng such counsel to take
As knyȝtez in cauelaciounz on Crystmasse gomnez!'
Wel much watz þe warme water þat waltered of yȝen,
When þat semly syre soȝt fro þo wonez    685
            þad daye.
        He made non abode,
        Bot wyȝtly went hys way;
        Mony wylsum way he rode,
        Þe bok as I herde say.    690

Now ridez þis renk þurȝ þe ryalme of Logres,
Sir Gauan, on Godez halue, þaȝ hym no gomen þoȝt.
Oft leudlez alone he lengez on nyȝtez
Þer he fonde noȝt hym byfore þe fare þat he lyked.
Hade he no fere bot his fole bi frythez and dounez,    695
Ne no gome bot God bi gate wyth to karp,
Til þat he neȝed ful neghe into þe Norþe Walez.

And bade them all good day
And set out for evermore.

He set spurs to his horse and sprang on his way
With such force that sparks flew from the stone behind him.
All who were watching that glorious knight sighed in their hearts,
And they all spoke mournfully to each other,
Grieving for that fair person: "By Christ, what a calamity
That you should be lost, Prince, whose life is so noble!
In faith it is not easy to find his equal upon earth.
It would have been wiser to proceed more prudently
And to have given that noble knight a dukedom to govern.
He would have made a great lord in the country,
And better that than being cut into nothing,
Beheaded by some creature from elfland because of vain pride.
Who ever heard of a king heeding such counsel
Among the court mummeries in the Christmas season?"
Many warm tears welled out of their eyes
When that fine lord went out of the house
           that day.
     He lodged nowhere
     But pressed ahead on his way,
     Which was foreign and far,
     As I heard the book say.

*[handwritten margin note: Now they disapprove — want him to break my oath]*

Now this knight rides through the realm of Logres:
Sir Gawain, in God's name, and it was no game for him.
Many nights he spends by himself, with no one,
Without having the food he likes set down before him.
He had no company but his horse through the woods and over the hills,
And no one but God to talk with on his way,
Until he had nearly come into North Wales.

Alle þe iles of Anglesay on lyft half he haldez,
And farez ouer þe fordez by þe forlondez,
Ouer at þe Holy Hede, til he hade eft bonk         700
In þe wyldrenesse of Wyrale; wonde þer bot lyte
Þat auþer God oþer gome wyth goud hert louied.
And ay he frayned, as he ferde, at frekez þat he met,
If þay hade herde any karp of a knyȝt grene,
In any grounde þeraboute, of þe grene chapel;      705
And al nykked hym wyth nay, þat neuer in her lyue
Þay seȝe neuer no segge þat watz of suche hwez
      of grene.
        Þe knyȝt tok gates straunge
        In mony a bonk vnbene,      710
        His cher ful oft con chaunge
        Þat chapel er he myȝt sene.

Mony klyf he ouerclambe in contrayez straunge,
Fer floten fro his frendez fremedly he rydez.
At vche warþe oþer water þer þe wyȝe passed      715
He fonde a foo hym byfore, bot ferly hit were,
And þat so foule and so felle þat feȝt hym byhode.
So mony meruayl bi mount þer þe mon fyndez,
Hit were to tore for to telle of þe tenþe dole.
Sumwhyle wyth wormez he werrez, and with wolues als,   720
Sumwhyle wyth wodwos, þat woned in þe knarrez,
Boþe wyth bullez and berez, and borez oþerquyle,
And etaynez, þat hym anelede of þe heȝe felle;
Nade he ben duȝty and dryȝe, and Dryȝtyn had serued,
Douteles he hade ben ded and dreped ful ofte.     725
For werre wrathed hym not so much þat wynter nas wors,
When þe colde cler water fro þe cloudez schadde,
And fres er hit falle myȝt to þe fale erþe;

He has all the isles of Anglesey to the left of him
And rides across the fords between the headlands
Over by Holyhead, and out on the far shore,
Into the wilderness of Wirral, where there were few living
Who had love at all for God or anyone.
And always as he went he asked whoever he met
Whether they had ever heard tell of a Green Knight
Anywhere in that country, or of the Green Chapel,
And they all said no to him, and that never in their lives
Had they ever seen anyone of a green color
   like that.
   The knight followed strange roads
   Across many a wild hill.
   He will pass through many moods
   Before he beholds that chapel.


Many crags he climbed across in wild places.
Far from his friends he rides, wandering as a stranger.
At each river bank, as the knight crossed another water,
It was a wonder if he did not find another foe facing him,
And so foul and fierce that he had to fight with it.
So many marvels the man met on those mountains
That it would be hard to tell the tenth part of it.
Sometimes he fights with dragons, and with wolves at other times,
Sometimes with trolls holed up in the crags,
And at other times with bulls and bears and wild boars
And ogres panting after him out of the wild cliff faces.
Had he not been strong and steadfast and in God's service,
Doubtless he would have been killed many times over, and done with.
It was not the fighting that afflicted him so much: the winter was worse
When the cold clear water poured out of the clouds
And froze before it could fall upon the pale earth.

Ner slayn wyth þe slete he sleped in his yrnes  
Mo ny3tez þen innoghe in naked rokkez, 730  
Þer as claterande fro þe crest þe colde borne rennez,  
And henged he3e ouer his hede in hard iisse-ikkles.  
Þus in peryl and payne and plytes ful harde  
Bi contray caryez þis kny3t, tyl Krystmasse euen,  
       al one; 735  
       Þe kny3t wel þat tyde  
       To Mary made his mone,  
       Þat ho hym red to ryde  
       And wysse hym to sum wone.

Bi a mounte on þe morne meryly he rydes 740  
Into a forest ful dep, þat ferly watz wylde,  
Hi3e hillez on vche a halue, and holtwodez vnder  
Of hore okez ful hoge a hundreth togeder;  
Þe hasel and þe ha3þorne were harled al samen,  
With ro3e raged mosse rayled aywhere, 745  
With mony bryddez vnblyþe vpon bare twyges,  
Þat pitosly þer piped for pyne of þe colde.  
Þe gome vpon Gryngolet glydez hem vnder,  
Þur3 mony misy and myre, mon al hym one,  
Carande for his costes, lest he ne keuer schulde 750  
To se þe seruyse of þat syre, þat on þat self ny3t  
Of a burde watz borne oure baret to quelle;  
And þerfore sykyng he sayde, 'I beseche þe, lorde,  
And Mary, þat is myldest moder so dere,  
Of sum herber þer he3ly I my3t here masse, 755  
Ande þy matynez to-morne, mekely I ask,  
And þerto prestly I pray my pater and aue  
       and crede.'

Nearly slain by the sleet he slept in his armor
Among naked rocks more than enough nights
Where the cold stream runs splashing down from the crest
And the hard icicles hung high over his head.
Thus in peril and hardship and the risk of his life
This knight rides through that region until Christmas Eve,
   alone.
  Then the knight devoutly
  Made his plaint to Mary, asking
  Her to guide him on his way
  And lead him to some dwelling.


In the morning, with a high heart he rides by a mountain
Into the depths of a forest so wild he marveled at it,
High hills all around him and woods on the hillsides,
Hoary oaks, huge ones, a hundred of them together.
The hazel and the hawthorn tangled in each other
With rough shaggy moss massed on them everywhere,
And many birds mournful on the bare twigs,
Piteously piping there from the pain of the cold.
The knight pushes on, beneath them, on Gryngolet,
Through many bogs and mires, all by himself,
Anxious about his devotions, for fear that he would fail
To observe that lord's service who on that same night
Was born of a maiden to end our suffering,
And so he said, sighing, "Lord, I beseech you,
And Mary, most tender, most precious of mothers,
For some house where I may hear Mass devoutly,
And your matins tomorrow morning; meekly I ask it
And for that pray here and now my Pater and Ave
   and Creed."

He rode in his prayere,
And cryed for his mysdede,         760
He sayned hym in syþes sere,
And sayde 'Cros Kryst me spede!'

Nade he sayned hymself, segge, bot þrye,
Er he watz war in þe wod of a won in a mote,
Abof a launde, on a lawe, loken vnder boȝez      765
Of mony borelych bole aboute bi þe diches:
A castel þe comlokest þat euer knyȝt aȝte,
Pyched on a prayere, a park al aboute,
With a pyked palays pyned ful þik,
Þat vmbeteȝe mony tre mo þen two myle.      770
Þat holde on þat on syde þe haþel auysed,
As hit schemered and schon þurȝ þe schyre okez;
Þenne hatz he hendly of his helme, and heȝly he þonkez
Jesus and sayn Gilyan, þat gentyle ar boþe,
Þat cortaysly had hym kydde, and his cry herkened.
'Now bone hostel,' coþe þe burne, 'I beseche yow ȝette!'    776
Þenne gerdez he to Gryngolet with þe gilt helez,
And he ful chauncely hatz chosen to þe chef gate,
Þat broȝt bremly þe burne to þe bryge ende
           in haste.      780
      Þe bryge watz breme vpbrayde,
      Þe ȝatez wer stoken faste,
      Þe wallez were wel arayed,
      Hit dut no wyndez blaste.

Þe burne bode on blonk, þat on bonk houed      785
Of þe depe double dich þat drof to þe place;
Þe walle wod in þe water wonderly depe,
Ande eft a ful huge heȝt hit haled vpon lofte

He rode on, praying, repenting
His misdeeds, and he
Kept crossing himself, saying,
"Cross of Christ, bless me!"

The knight had not crossed himself more than three times
When he saw through the forest a house inside a moat
Above a meadow, on a mound, shaded by the boughs
Of many massive trunks along the water's edge.
The loveliest castle that any knight ever had,
Built on a green, a park all around it
With a palisade of pikes planted on all sides
And many trees, for more than two miles around them.
The knight gazed at the side of the castle nearest to him,
Shimmering and shining through the gleaming oaks.
Then he takes off his helmet and devoutly thanks
Jesus and Saint Julian, both of whom are kind,
Who had heard his cry and answered him with kindness.
"Now I beg you," the knight said, "to grant me good lodging."
Then with his gilded heels he spurs Gryngolet
And by chance it was the main approach that he had found
And before long he arrived at the end
                of the drawbridge.
        The bridge was pulled up hard,
        The gates were shut fast.
        The walls were solid,
        Fearing no wind's blast.

Astride his horse, the knight waited on the bank
Of the deep double ditch that encircled the palace.
The wall went wonderfully deep into the water
And it rose to a huge height over him,

Of harde hewen ston vp to þe tablez,
Enbaned vnder þe abataylment in þe best lawe;    790
And syþen garytez ful gaye gered bitwene,
Wyth mony luflych loupe þat louked ful clene:
A better barbican þat burne blusched vpon neuer.
And innermore he behelde þat halle ful hyȝe,
Towres telded bytwene, trochet ful þik,    795
Fayre fylyolez þat fyȝed, and ferlyly long,
With coruon coprounes craftyly sleȝe.
Chalkwhyt chymnees þer ches he innoȝe
Vpon bastel rouez, þat blenked ful quyte;
So mony pynakle payntet watz poudred ayquere,    800
Among þe castel carnelez clambred so þik,
Þat pared out of papure purely hit semed.
Þe fre freke on þe fole hit fayr innoghe þoȝt,
If he myȝt keuer to com þe cloyster wythinne,
To herber in þat hostel whyl halyday lested,    805
                auinant.
      He calde, and sone þer com
      A porter pure plesaunt,
      On þe wal his ernd he nome,
      And haylsed þe knyȝt erraunt.    810

'Gode sir,' quoþ Gawan, 'woldez þou go myn ernde
To þe heȝ lorde of þis hous, herber to craue?'
'Ȝe, Peter,' quoþ þe porter, 'and purely I trowee
Þat ȝe be, wyȝe, welcum to won quyle yow lykez.'
Þen ȝede þe wyȝe ȝerne and com aȝayn swyþe,    815
And folke frely hym wyth, to fonge þe knyȝt.
Þay let doun þe grete draȝt and derely out ȝeden,
And kneled doun on her knes vpon þe colde erþe
To welcum þis ilk wyȝ as worþy hom þoȝt;

Of hard hewn stone up to the cornices,
With ledges stepped beneath the battlements in the best manner
And elegant watchtowers arranged at intervals
With many fine windows neatly locked shut.
Never had that knight beheld better defenses.
And he saw, farther inside that tall castle,
Towers rising around it, clustered with pinnacles,
Graceful spires set perfectly, their length a marvel,
With carvings at the tops of them artfully made.
And he could make out many chalk-white chimneys,
Their white gleaming over the roofs of the towers.
There were so many painted pinnacles all over it everywhere,
So densely arrayed among the castle battlements,
That they appeared to have been cut cleverly out of paper.
To the knight on his horse it seemed more than he had hoped for.
If he could make his way into that enclosure,
He would be happy to stay in that house
                    for the holiday.
          He called, and in a short while
          A porter came, perfectly polite,
          Who took up his post on the wall
          And greeted the questing knight.

*Another stop on hero's journey*

"Good sir," Gawain said, "will you be my messenger
To the lord of this house, to ask him for lodging here?"
"Yes, in Peter's name," the porter said, "and I am sure
That you will be welcome, Knight, for as long as you like."
Then before long that gentleman was back,
And others with him, to make the knight welcome.
They let down the great drawbridge and came out courteously
And knelt down on their knees upon the cold earth
To welcome this very man as they thought he deserved.

Þay ȝolden hym þe brode ȝate, ȝarked vp wyde,                    820
And he hem raysed rekenly, and rod ouer þe brygge.
Sere seggez hym sesed by sadel, quel he lyȝt,
And syþen stabeled his stede stif men innoȝe.
Knyȝtez and swyerez comen doun þenne
For to bryng þis buurne wyth blys into halle;                    825
Quen he hef vp his helme, þer hiȝed innoghe
For to hent hit at his honde, þe hende to seruen;
His bronde and his blasoun boþe þay token.
Þen haylsed he ful hendly þo haþelez vchone,
And mony proud mon þer presed þat prynce to honour.             830
Alle hasped in his heȝ wede to halle þay hym wonnen,
Þer fayre fyre vpon flet fersly brenned.
Þenne þe lorde of þe lede loutez fro his chambre
For to mete wyth menske þe mon on þe flor;
He sayde, 'Ȝe ar welcum to welde as yow lykez                   835
Þat here is; al is yowre awen, to haue at yowre wylle
        and welde.'
      'Graunt mercy,' quoþ Gawayn,
      'Þer Kryst hit yow forȝelde.'
      As frekez þat semed fayn                           840
      Ayþer oþer in armez con felde.

Gawayn glyȝt on þe gome þat godly hym gret,
And þuȝt hit a bolde burne þat þe burȝ aȝte,
A hoge haþel for þe nonez, and of hyghe eldee;
Brode, bryȝt, watz his berde, and al beuer-hwed,               845
Sturne, stif on þe stryþþe on stalworth schonkez,
Felle face as þe fyre, and fre of hys speche;
And wel hym semed, for soþe, as þe segge þuȝt,
To lede a lortschyp in lee of leudez ful gode.
Þe lorde hym charred to a chambre, and chefly cumaundez

They led him in by the broad gate, opened up wide,
And he told them to stand, and he rode over the bridge.
Many hands held his saddle while he dismounted,
And many strong men led his horse to the stable.
Then knights and squires gathered around him
To escort this knight joyfully into the hall.
When he raised his helmet they hurried to him
To take it from his hand, waiting upon him.
His sword and his shield, both of them, were taken.
Then he greeted each one of the knights there graciously,
And many proud men pressed forward to honor that prince.
All clad in his armor they brought him to the hall,
Where a fine fire was burning fiercely.
Then the lord of them all comes from his chamber
To greet the man in the hall with honor.
He said, "You are welcome to use this house as you will.
Everything here is your own, for your pleasure
       and use."
      Gawain said, "God grant you mercy,
      The Christ reward your care."
      Then as knights, heartily,
      They embraced each other.

Gawain looked at the man who welcomed him so warmly
And thought he was a bold knight who held this castle.
A huge warrior indeed, and in the prime of life,
Broad, and his beard was bright, and beaver-red.
He was formidable, standing firm on stalwart legs,
Face fierce as the fire, and free with his speech.
He seemed well suited, certainly, the knight thought,
To be lord of a castle and of good people.
The lord led him to a chamber and gave careful orders

To delyuer hym a leude, hym loȝly to serue;                      851
And þere were boun at his bode burnez innoȝe,
Þat broȝt hym to a bryȝt boure, þer beddyng watz noble,
Of cortynes of clene sylk wyth cler golde hemmez,
And couertorez ful curious with comlych panez                    855
Of bryȝt blaunner aboue, enbrawded bisydez,
Rudelez rennande on ropez, red golde ryngez,
Tapitez tyȝt to þe woȝe of tuly and tars,
And vnder fete, on þe flet, of folȝande sute.
Þer he watz dispoyled, wyth spechez of myerþe,                   860
Þe burn of his bruny and of his bryȝt wedez.
Ryche robes ful rad renkkez hym broȝten,
For to charge, and to chaunge, and chose of þe best.
Sone as he on hent, and happed þerinne,
Þat sete on hym semly wyth saylande skyrtez,                     865
Þe ver by his uisage verayly hit semed
Welneȝ to vche haþel, alle on hwes
Lowande and lufly alle his lymmez vnder,
Þat a comloker knyȝt neuer Kryst made
      hem þoȝt.                      870
    Wheþen in worlde he were,
    Hit semed as he moȝt
    Be prynce withouten pere
    In felde þer felle men foȝt.

A cheyer byfore þe chemné, þer charcole brenned,                 875
Watz grayþed for Sir Gawan grayþely with cloþez,
Whyssynes vpon queldepoyntes þat koynt wer boþe;
And þenne a meré mantyle watz on þat mon cast
Of a broun bleeaunt, enbrauded ful ryche
And fayre furred wythinne with fellez of þe best,                880
Alle of ermyn in erde, his hode of þe same;

[ 60 ]

For someone to be assigned to serve Gawain,
And at his bidding a number of knights
Conducted him to a bright bedroom with noble bedclothes,
Curtains of pure silk with shining gold hems
And elaborate coverlets with elegant panels
Of white fur with embroidery around them,
Curtains running on cords, with red gold rings,
Tapestries on the wall from Tharsia and Toulouse
And more of the same under foot on the floor.
There they took off his gear, talking and laughing,
His knight's shirt of mail, his bright armor and garments.
They had rich robes fit for a prince ready for him
To take in exchange, choosing what he liked best.
As soon as he had them and had put them on,
They suited him beautifully with their long falls,
And surely it looked almost as though spring had come,
To each knight there, with the colors of the clothes,
Bright and beautiful, and his limbs inside them.
Christ never made a more splendid knight,
            they thought.
        It seemed to them that wherever
        In the world he came from, he might
        Be a prince without peer
        In the field where bold men fight.


Before the fireplace, where charcoal was burning,
A chair was placed for Gawain, with coverings over it:
Cushions on quilts, both of them beautiful,
And then a rich mantle was cast around him
Of an elegant brown fabric lavishly embroidered
And neatly lined with the finest of furs,
All trimmed with ermine, and his hood was the same,

And he sete in þat settel semlych ryche,
And achaufed hym chefly, and þenne his cher mended.
Sone watz telded vp a tabil on trestez ful fayre,
Clad wyth a clene cloþe þat cler quyt schewed,                          885
Sanap, and salure, and syluerin sponez.
Þe wyʒe wesche at his wylle, and went to his mete.
Seggez hym serued semly innoʒe
Wyth sere sewes and sete, sesounde of þe best,
Double-felde, as hit fallez, and fele kyn fischez,                        890
Summe baken in bred, summe brad on þe gledez,
Summe soþen, summe in sewe sauered with spyces,
And ay sawes so sleʒe þat þe segge lyked.
Þe freke calde hit a fest ful frely and ofte
Ful hendely, quen alle þe haþeles rehayted hym at onez,          895
      'As hende,
        Þis penaunce now ʒe take,
        And eft hit schal amende.'
        Þat mon much merþe con make,
        For wyn in his hed þat wende.                              900

Þenne watz spyed and spured vpon spare wyse
Bi preué poyntez of þat prynce, put to hymseluen,
Þat he beknew cortaysly of þe court þat he were
Þat aþel Arthure þe hende haldez hym one,
Þat is þe ryche ryal kyng of þe Rounde Table,                           905
And hit watz Wawen hymself þat in þat won syttez,
Comen to þat Krystmasse, as case hym þen lymped.
When þe lorde hade lerned þat he þe leude hade,
Loude laʒed he þerat, so lef hit hym þoʒt,
And alle þe men in þat mote maden much joye                          910
To apere in his presense prestly þat tyme,
Þat alle prys and prowes and pured þewes

And he sat in that seat, lapped in splendor,
And warmed himself well, and his spirits rose.
Soon they set up a table on handsome trestles
Covered with a cloth of pure gleaming white,
Napkins on top of it, and a salt cellar and silver spoons.
He washed at his leisure and went to his food.
There were many servers to wait upon him
With a choice of fine dishes wonderfully seasoned,
Double portions, for the occasion, and many kinds of fish,
Some baked in bread, some grilled on the embers,
Some boiled, some in stews flavored with spices,
And all the rich sauces that the man liked.
The knight kept politely calling it a feast
With the lords all urging him on together
        as he ate:
      "This penance now you suffer
      For better things to come."
      He moved them to much laughter
      As the wine rose in him.


Then tactfully they brought the question around,
Asking that prince discreetly about himself,
And he confessed courteously that he had come from the court
Which the noble Arthur ruled alone by his grace,
The most royal King of the Round Table,
And that he himself, sitting in that hall, was Gawain,
Come there for Christmas as chance had guided him.
When the lord learned who the prince was, there with them,
He laughed aloud, it made him so happy,
And all the men in that castle showed their joy
At being there in his presence at that moment,
For every virtue and all valor and chivalry

Apendes to hys persoun, and praysed is euer;
Byfore alle men vpon molde his mensk is þe most.
Vch segge ful softly sayde to his fere:                    915
'Now schal we semlych se sleȝtez of þewez
And þe teccheles termes of talkyng noble,
Wich spede is in speche vnspurd may we lerne,
Syn we haf fonged þat fyne fader of nurture.
God hatz geuen vus his grace godly for soþe,              920
Þat such a gest as Gawan grauntez vus to haue,
When burnez blyþe of his burþe schal sitte
            and synge.
        In menyng of manerez mere
        Þis burne now schal vus bryng,
        I hope þat may hym here                          926
        Schal lerne of luf-talkyng.'


Bi þat þe diner watz done and þe dere vp
Hit watz neȝ at þe niyȝt neȝed þe tyme.
Chaplaynez to þe chapeles chosen þe gate,                930
Rungen ful rychely, ryȝt as þay schulden,
To þe hersum euensong of þe hyȝe tyde.
Þe lorde loutes þerto, and þe lady als,
Into a cumly closet coyntly ho entrez.
Gawan glydez ful gay and gos þeder sone;                 935
Þe lorde laches hym by þe lappe and ledez hym to sytte,
And couþly hym knowez and callez hym his nome,
And sayde he watz þe welcomest wyȝe of þe worlde;
And he hym þonkked þroly, and ayþer halched oþer,
And seten soberly samen þe seruise quyle.                940
Þenne lyst þe lady to loke on þe knyȝt,
Þenne com ho of hir closet with mony cler burdez.
Ho watz þe fayrest in felle, of flesche and of lyre,

Were said to be his and were praised constantly,
He was honored above all other men on earth.
Each knight murmured quietly to his companion,
"Now we shall see displays of elegant manners
And hear pure examples of noble expression.
We may learn the best forms of speech without asking,
Since our guest is that refined scion of courtliness.
God has indeed been bountiful to us with his grace
To have granted us such a guest as Gawain
To be here at the time of Christ's birth, when the knights will sit
      and sing.
      This knight will lead us
      To understand noble manners.
      I hope that all of us
      May learn the language of lovers."


And then the dinner was done and the guest standing.
It was the time when the night was drawing near.
Chaplains were on their way to the chapels,
The bells ringing joyfully as rightly they should
For the solemn evensong of the high festival.
The lord turns to these devotions, and the lady too,
And she steps gracefully into a fine enclosed compartment.
Gawain, striding happily, is soon there.
The lord takes his sleeve and leads him to a seat
And speaks to him as a friend, calling him by his name,
Saying he was more welcome than anyone in the world.
Gawain thanked him heartily and they embraced each other
And sat together soberly all through the service.
Then it pleased the lady to look at the knight
As she stepped from her pew with many lovely maidens.
She was more fair of skin, of cheek and of flesh,

And of compas and colour and costes, of alle oþer,
And wener þen Wenore, as þe wyȝe þoȝt.                         945
Ho ches þurȝ þe chaunsel to cheryche þat hende.
An oþer lady hir lad bi þe lyft honde,
Þat watz alder þen ho, an auncian hit semed,
And heȝly honowred with haþelez aboute.
Bot vnlyke on to loke þo ladyes were,                         950
For if þe ȝonge watz ȝep, ȝolȝe watz þat oþer;
Riche red on þat on rayled ayquere,
Rugh ronkled chekez þat oþer on rolled;
Kerchofes of þat on, wyth mony cler perlez,
Hir brest and hir bryȝt þrote bare displayed,                 955
Schon schyrer þen snawe þat schedez on hillez;
Þat oþer wyth a gorger watz gered ouer þe swyre,
Chymbled ouer hir blake chyn with chalkquyte vayles,
Hir frount folden in sylk, enfoubled ayquere,
Toreted and treleted with tryflez aboute,                     960
Þat noȝt watz bare of þat burde bot þe blake broȝes,
Þe tweyne yȝen and þe nase, þe naked lyppez,
And þose were soure to se and sellyly blered;
A mensk lady on molde mon may hir calle,
                  for Gode!                                    965
            Hir body watz schort and þik,
            Hir buttokez balȝ and brode,
            More lykkerwys on to lyk
            Watz þat scho hade on lode.


When Gawayn glyȝt on þat gay, þat graciously loked,           970
Wyth leue laȝt of þe lorde he lent hem aȝaynes;
Þe alder he haylses, heldande ful lowe,
Þe loueloker he lappez a lyttel in armez,
He kysses hir comlyly, and knyȝtly he melez.

Of figure and color and manner, than any of them,
More beautiful, it seemed to the knight, than Guenever.
He made his way to the chancel to greet her grace.
Another lady was leading her by the left hand,
Who was older than she was; she seemed ancient,
And was treated with much honor by the knights around her,
But those two ladies were not alike to look at,
For where the young one was fresh the other was withered;
Clear pink was that one's color everywhere;
Rough wrinkled cheeks hung down on the other.
Kerchiefs on that one, with many gleaming pearls,
Adorned her breast and her bare white throat
Brighter than snow that falls on the hills.
That other was wearing a scarf around her neck
Wrapped across her black chin, with chalk-white veils
And a silk muffler folded over her forehead,
Knotted up into turrets and tricked out with ornaments
So that nothing of that lady showed but the black eyebrows,
The two eyes and the nose, the naked lips,
And those were unpleasant to look at and watery.
A great lady on earth, one would have to admit,
       before God!
    Her body was short and wide,
    Her buttocks round and broad.
    One would rather have tasted
    The other one whom she led.


When Gawain had gazed at that beauty and her gracious glances,
With the lord's leave he went over to the ladies.
He greeted the elder one with a low bow.
The lovelier one he embraced lightly,
Kissed her politely, and addressed her in courtly fashion.

Þay kallen hym of aquoyntaunce, and he hit quyk askez          975
To be her seruaunt sothly, if hemself lyked.
Þay tan hym bytwene hem, wyth talkyng hym leden
To chambre, to chemné, and chefly þay asken
Spycez, þat vnsparely men speded hom to bryng,
And þe wynnelych wyne þerwith vche tyme.          980
Þe lorde luflych aloft lepez ful ofte,
Mynned merthe to be made vpon mony syþez,
Hent heȝly of his hode, and on a spere henged,
And wayned hom to wynne þe worchip þerof,
Þat most myrþe myȝt meue þat Crystenmas whyle—          985
'And I schal fonde, bi my fayth, to fylter wyth þe best
Er me wont þe wede, with help of my frendez.'
Þus wyth laȝande lotez þe lorde hit tayt makez,
For to glade Sir Gawayn with gomnez in halle
          þat nyȝt,          990
     Til þat hit watz tyme
     Þe lord comaundet lyȝt;
     Sir Gawen his leue con nyme
     And to his bed hym diȝt.

On þe morne, as vch mon mynez þat tyme          995
Þat Dryȝtyn for oure destyné to deȝe watz borne,
Wele waxez in vche a won in worlde for his sake;
So did hit þere on þat day þurȝ dayntés mony:
Boþe at mes and at mele messes ful quaynt
Derf men vpon dece drest of þe best.          1000
Þe olde auncian wyf heȝest ho syttez,
Þe lorde lufly her by lent, as I trowe;
Gawan and þe gay burde togeder þay seten,
Euen inmyddez, as þe messe metely come,
And syþen þurȝ al þe sale as hem best semed.          1005

They ask to be acquainted and at once he requests
To be their true servant, if that would please them.
They took him between them and led him, while they talked,
To a chamber and a fireplace, and they sent at once
For spices, which servants brought them without stinting,
And with them the fine wine, every time they came.
The lord kept leaping lightly to his feet
Saying things to them that made them laugh.
He took off his hood, in play, and hung it on a spear,
Waving it as a prize for whoever was able
To amuse them most at that Christmas season—
"And by my faith, I shall match myself with the best
Before my friends help me to lose this headpiece."
So with words and laughter the lord entertains them
To amuse Sir Gawain among the nobles in the hall,
                    that night.
            Until the lord sent for light
            When it was needed,
            And Gawain said his good night
            And went off to his bed.


In the morning, as each one thought of the time
When God was born to die for our destiny,
Joy welled up in everyone in this world because of him.
So it did there on that day, with many pleasures,
The choicest of dishes at every meal,
An array of the best for the nobles at the high table.
The ancient woman sits in the highest seat.
The lord took his place next to her politely, believe me.
Gawain and the lovely lady sit together
At the middle of the table, and the meal was properly served,
Each servant, all through the hall then, bringing

Bi vche grome at his degré grayþely watz serued
Þer watz mete, þer watz myrþe, þer watz much ioye,
Þat for to telle þerof hit me tene were,
And to poynte hit ȝet I pyned me parauenture.
Bot ȝet I wot þat Wawen and þe wale burde                    1010
Such comfort of her compaynye caȝten togeder
Þurȝ her dere dalyaunce of her derne wordez,
Wyth clene cortays carp closed fro fylþe,
Þat hor play watz passande vche prynce gomen,
      in vayres.                                         1015
        Trumpez and nakerys,
        Much pypyng þer repayres;
        Vche mon tented hys,
        And þay two tented þayres.

Much dut watz þer dryuen þat day and þat oþer,              1020
And þe þryd as þro þronge in þerafter;
Þe ioye of sayn Jonez day watz gentyle to here,
And watz þe last of þe layk, leudez þer þoȝten.
Þer wer gestes to go vpon þe gray morne,
Forþy wonderly þay woke, and þe wyn dronken,               1025
Daunsed ful dreȝly wyth dere carolez.
At þe last, when hit watz late, þay lachen her leue,
Vchon to wende on his way þat watz wyȝe stronge.
Gawan gef hym god day, þe godmon hym lachchez,
Ledes hym to his awen chambre, þe chymné bysyde,           1030
And þere he draȝez hym on dryȝe, and derely hym þonkkez
Of þe wynne worschip þat he hym wayued hade,
As to honour his hous on þat hyȝe tyde,
And enbelyse his burȝ with his bele chere:
'Iwysse sir, quyl I leue, me worþez þe better               1035

Everyone, according to his rank, what he wanted.
There was food, there was laughter, there was much joy
So that I would be hard put to tell of it
And to describe it even if I did my best to.
But well I know that Gawain and the fair lady
Took such comfort in each other's company,
In courtly conversation privately exchanged,
Pure polite talk free from any lewdness,
That their play surpassed every princely pleasure,
    so much is certain.
   Trumpets and kettledrums
   And many pipes played there.
   Everyone listens
   And those two hear each other.

Much joy they all had through that day and the next
And the third one was as crowded with pleasures.
The joy of Saint John's Day had a gentler sound,
Since it was the last day of the feast, as they all remembered.
There were guests who would go away in the gray morning.
So they stayed up and drank wine far into the night
And danced without stopping, to the steps of pretty carols.
At last, when it was late, they took their leave,
Each sturdy knight setting off on his own way.
Gawain wishes them good day and his good host takes hold of him
And leads him to his own chamber, up to the fireplace,
Where he draws him aside and thanks him warmly
For the great favor that he had bestowed upon him
In honoring his house at that high season
And gracing his castle with his noble spirit.
"I am sure, sire, while I live, that I shall be the better

Þat Gawayn hatz ben my gest at Goddez awen fest.'
'Grant merci, sir,' quoþ Gawayn, 'in god fayth hit is yowrez,
Al þe honour is your awen—þe heȝe kyng yow ȝelde!
And I am wyȝe at your wylle to worch youre hest,
As I am halden þerto, in hyȝe and in loȝe,       1040
      bi riȝt.'
        Þe lorde fast can hym payne
        To holde lenger þe knyȝt;
        To hym answarez Gawayn
        Bi non way þat he myȝt.       1045

Then frayned þe freke ful fayre at himseluen
Quat derue dede had hym dryuen at þat dere tyme
So kenly fro þe kyngez kourt to kayre al his one,
Er þe halidayez holly were halet out of toun.
'For soþe, sir,' quoþ þe segge, 'ȝe sayn bot þe trawþe,     1050
A heȝe ernde and a hasty me hade fro þo wonez,
For I am sumned myselfe to sech to a place,
I ne wot in worlde whederwarde to wende hit to fynde.
I nolde bot if I hit negh myȝt on Nw ȝeres morne
For alle þe londe inwyth Logres, so me oure lorde help!     1055
Forþy, sir, þis enquest I require yow here,
Þat ȝe me telle with trawþe if euer ȝe tale herde
Of þe grene chapel, quere hit on grounde stondez,
And of þe knyȝt þat hit kepes, of colour of grene.
Þer watz stabled bi statut a steuen vus bytwene     1060
To mete þat mon at þat mere, ȝif I myȝt last;
And of þat ilk Nw ȝere bot neked now wontez,
And I wolde loke on þat lede, if God me let wolde,
Gladloker, bi Goddez sun, þen any god welde!
Forþi, iwysse, bi ȝowre wylle, wende me bihoues,     1065

For having had Gawain as my guest at God's own feast."
"My thanks to you, sir," Gawain said, "and in good faith
The honor is all your own—may the High King reward you!
And I pledge myself to your will, to do your bidding,
As I am bound to, in matters great and small,
> by right."
>> The lord urges
>> The knight to stay
>> But Gawain replies
>> That it cannot be.


Then the lord asked him courteously
What grim deed had driven him, at that season of celebration,
From the King's court, to set out so boldly, all alone,
Before the holidays were over in the houses.
"To tell the truth, sir," the knight said, "and the plain truth,
A high and compelling mission called me away,
For I alone have been summoned to find a place
I do not know where in the world to look for.
I would not fail to be there on New Year's morning
For all the land in Logres, the Lord help me find it!
To that end, sir, I put this question to you:
Tell me the truth: have you ever heard
Of the Green Chapel, where it stands on the earth,
And of the knight who guards it, who is of a green color?
There was a solemn appointment settled between us
For me to meet that man there if I lived that long,
And now until that New Year there remains almost nothing,
And I would rather set eyes on that knight, if God will let me,
By God's sun, than have any fine thing.
And so indeed, with your permission, I must be on my way,

Naf I now to busy bot bare þre dayez,
And me als fayn to falle feye as fayly of myyn ernde.'
Þenne laȝande quoþ þe lorde, 'Now leng þe byhoues,
For I schal teche yow to þat terme bi þe tymez ende,
Þe grene chapayle vpon grounde greue yow no more;          1070
Bot ȝe schal be in yowre bed, burne, at þyn ese,
Quyle forth dayez, and ferk on þe fyrst of þe ȝere,
And cum to þat merk at mydmorn, to make quat yow likez
   in spenne.
    Dowellez whyle New ȝeres daye,          1075
    And rys, and raykez þenne,
    Mon schal yow sette in waye,
    Hit is not two myle henne.'


Þenne watz Gawan ful glad, and gomenly he laȝed:
'Now I þonk yow þryuandely þurȝ alle oþer þynge,          1080
Now acheued is my chaunce, I schal at your wylle
Dowelle, and ellez do quat ȝe demen.'
Þenne sesed hym þe syre and set hym bysyde,
Let þe ladiez be fette to lyke hem þe better.
Þer watz seme solace by hemself stille;          1085
Þe lorde let for luf lotez so myry,
As wyȝ þat wolde of his wyte, ne wyst quat he myȝt.
Þenne he carped to þe knyȝt, criande loude,
'Ȝe han demed to do þe dede þat I bidde;
Wyl ȝe halde þis hes here at þys onez?'          1090
'Ȝe, sir, for soþe,' sayd þe segge trwe,
'Whyl I byde in yowre borȝe, be bayn to ȝowre hest.'
'For ȝe haf trauayled,' quoþ þe tulk, 'towen fro ferre,
And syþen waked me wyth, ȝe arn not wel waryst
Nauþer of sostnaunce ne of slepe, soþly I knowe;          1095

Since I have barely three days left now to find it,
And it would be better to die than to fail in my mission."
Then the lord said, laughing, "Now you must stay on here,
For I shall tell you how to find that place before the time is up.
Grieve no longer over where on earth the Green Chapel is,
For you will be in your bed, Knight, at your ease
Well into the day, and ride out on the first of the year
And come to that spot in mid-morning to do as you please
        at that place.
      Stay on until New Year's Day
      And rise and take your leave then.
      You will be shown the way.
      It is less than two miles farther on."

Then Gawain was glad, and he laughed happily.
"Now I thank you heartily for this, beyond all the rest.
Now my quest is accomplished, and I shall stay
As you wish, and do whatever else you may ask."
Then the sire took hold of him and sat beside him
And sent for the ladies to entertain him.
There by themselves they lingered at their pleasure.
The lord talked happily as a friend to a friend,
Someone not overwatchful in his words,
And he said to the knight, his voice rising,
"You have sworn to do whatever I ask.
Will you keep that promise here and now?"
The true knight answered, "Truly, sir, I will obey
Your wishes while I stay in your castle."
"Since you have traveled hard," the lord said, "coming so far,
And then dined late with me, you are not well restored yet
Either with food or sleep, I am sure of it.

Ʒe schal lenge in your lofte, and lyʒe in your ese
To-morn quyle þe messequyle, and to mete wende
When ʒe wyl, wyth my wyf, þat wyth yow schal sitte
And comfort yow with compayny, til I to cort torne;
        Ʒe lende,             1100
        And I schal erly ryse,
        On huntyng wyl I wende.'
        Gauayn grantez alle þyse,
        Hym heldande, as þe hende.

'Ʒet firre,' quoþ þe freke, 'a forwarde we make:    1105
Quat-so-euer I wynne in þe wod hit worþez to yourez,
And quat chek so ʒe acheue chaunge me þerforne.
Swete, swap we so, sware with trawþe,
Queþer, leude, so lymp, lere oþer better.'
'Bi God,' quoþ Gawayn þe gode, 'I grant þertylle,    1110
And þat yow lyst for to layke, lef hit me þynkes.'
'Who bryngez vus þis beuerage, þis bargayn is maked':
So sayde þe lorde of þat lede; þay laʒed vchone,
Þay dronken and daylyeden and dalten vntyʒtel,
Þise lordez and ladyez, quyle þat hem lyked;    1115
And syþen with Frenkysch fare and fele fayre lotez
Þay stoden and stemed and stylly speken,
Kysten ful comlyly and kaʒten her leue.
With mony leude ful lyʒt and lemande torches
Vche burne to his bed watz broʒt at þe laste,    1125
    ful softe.
        To bed ʒet er þay ʒede,
        Recorded couenauntez ofte;
        Þe olde lorde of þat leude
        Cowþe wel halde layk alofte.    1125

You shall stay in your chamber and lie at your ease
Tomorrow until Mass time, and come for your meals
When you please, and my wife will sit next to you
And entertain you with her company until I come home.

                You stay
        And I shall rise early
        And be off hunting."
        Gawain grants this completely,
        Politely bowing.


"Besides, sir," the lord said, "let us have an agreement,
Whatever I take in the wood will be yours,
And in exchange you will give me whatever you may acquire.
Agree to that, good sir, and let us swear to it,
Whatever gain or loss may befall us."
"In God's name," good Gawain said, "I will grant you that,
And I am glad that you are a gambling man."
"Let us have a drink to seal our agreement,"
The lord said to that knight, and both of them laughed.
They drank and amused each other with their talk,
Those lords and ladies, at their leisure,
And then in courtly fashion and with many fine phrases
They stood lingering, speaking in low voices,
And kissed courteously and took leave of each other,
And, escorted by many servants with torches flaming,
Each knight was lighted at last to his
                soft bed.
        On their way to bed
        They went over their bargain.
        The castle's old lord
        Knew how to amuse them.

# III

Ful erly bifore þe day þe folk vprysen,
Gestes þat go wolde hor gromez þay calden,
And þay busken vp bilyue blonkkez to sadel,
Tyffen her takles, trussen her males,
Richen hem þe rychest, to ryde alle arayde,                     1130
Lepen vp ly3tly, lachen her brydeles,
Vche wy3e on his way þer hym wel lyked.
Þe leue lorde of þe londe watz not þe last
Arayed for þe rydyng, with renkkez ful mony;
Ete a sop hastyly, when he hade herde masse,                    1135
With bugle to bent-felde he buskez bylyue.
By þat any dayly3t lemed vpon erþe
He with his haþeles on hy3e horsses weren.
Þenne þise cacheres þat couþe cowpled hor houndez,
Vnclosed þe kenel dore and calde hem þeroute,                   1140
Blwe bygly in buglez þre bare mote;
Braches bayed þerfore and breme noyse maked;
And þay chastysed and charred on chasyng þat went,
A hundreth of hunteres, as I haf herde telle,
       of þe best.                                              1145
      To trystors vewters 3od,
      Couples huntes of kest;
      Þer ros for blastez gode
      Gret rurd in þat forest.

# III

Early, before daybreak, everyone was up.
The guests who were leaving summoned their servants
And they hurried to have the horses saddled,
Get their gear ready and their bags packed.
Dressed in high attire to ride in their finery,
They leap up lightly, take hold of their bridles,
Each heading off the way he wanted to go.
The belovèd lord of the land was not the last,
Dressed up for riding, many knights with him.
He eats something quickly when he has heard Mass.
With bugles blowing he hurries to the hunt.
By the time the daylight shone over the earth
He and his knights were on their tall horses.
The dog handlers skillfully leashed the hounds in pairs,
Unlocked the kennel door and called them out,
Blew loud on the bugles three bare notes
To start the hounds baying and raising a wild din,
And they whipped them in as they went off to the hunt,
A hundred hunters of the best, is the way
        I have heard it.
     Handlers went to their stations,
     Unleashed the paired hounds.
     The loud horns
     Filled the forest with their sounds.

At þe fyrst quethe of þe quest quaked þe wylde; 1150
Der drof in þe dale, doted for drede,
Hiȝed to þe hyȝe, bot heterly þay were
Restayed with þe stablye, þat stoutly ascryed.
Þay let þe herttez haf þe gate, with þe hyȝe hedes,
Þe breme bukkez also with hor brode paumez; 1155
For þe fre lorde hade defende in fermysoun tyme
Þat þer schulde no mon meue to þe male dere.
Þe hindez were halden in with hay! and war!
Þe does dryuen with gret dyn to þe depe sladez;
Þer myȝt mon se, as þay slypte, slentyng of arwes— 1160
At vche wende vnder wande wapped a flone—
Þat bigly bote on þe broun with ful brode hedez.
What! þay brayen, and bleden, bi bonkkez þay deȝen,
And ay rachches in a res radly hem folȝes,
Hunterez wyth hyȝe horne hasted hem after 1165
Wyth such a crakkande kry as klyffes haden brusten.
What wylde so atwaped wyȝes þat schotten
Watz al toraced and rent at þe resayt,
Bi þay were tened at þe hyȝe and taysed to þe wattrez;
Þe ledez were so lerned at þe loȝe trysteres, 1170
And þe grehoundez so grete, þat geten hem bylyue
And hem tofylched, as fast as frekez myȝt loke,
     þer-ryȝt.
      Þe lorde for blys abloy
      Ful oft con launce and lyȝt, 1175
      And drof þat day wyth joy
      Thus to þe derk nyȝt.

Þus laykez þis lorde by lynde-wodez euez,
And Gawayn þe god mon in gay bed lygez,
Lurkkez quyl þe daylyȝt lemed on þe wowes, 1180

[ 80 ]

When they first heard the hunt the wild creatures quaked.
Deer dashed to the hollows, dazed with dread,
Raced up to the ridges, but all at once they were
Turned back by the beaters and their loud shouts.
They let the harts pass on, holding their heads high,
And the brave bucks too, with their broad antlers,
Because the noble lord had forbidden anyone
To shoot at the stags during the closed season.
The hinds were held back with "Hey!" and with " 'Ware!,"
The does driven with all the din into the deep valleys.
There might a man see the loosed arrows flying,
The shafts flashing through every break in the forest.
The broad heads bit deep into the brown hides.
Look! They cry and bleed, they die on the hillsides,
And always the hounds are racing at their heels
And hunters with loud horns following behind them,
Their shouts sounding as though the cliffs were cracking.
Whatever wild creatures escaped the archers
Were pulled down and torn apart at the dog stations.
They were harried from the high places and driven to the water.
The beaters were so skillful at the stations down there,
And the greyhounds so huge and hard upon them
They snatched them down more swiftly than a man's eye
        could follow.
      The lord, wild with joy,
      Would race ahead, then alight,
      Happy that whole day
      And on to the dark night.

Thus this lord sports in the nearby forest
And Gawain, the good man, lies in his lovely bed
Staying snug while the daylight climbs on the walls,

Vnder couertour ful clere, cortyned aboute;
And as in slomeryng he slode, sle3ly he herde
A littel dyn at his dor, and dernly vpon;
And he heuez vp his hed out of þe cloþes,
A corner of þe cortyn he ca3t vp a lyttel,
And waytez warly þiderwarde quat hit be my3t.                    1186
Hit watz þe ladi, loflyest to beholde,
Þat dro3 þe dor after hir ful dernly and stylle,
And bo3ed towarde þe bed; and þe burne schamed,
And layde hym doun lystyly, and let as he slepte;              1190
And ho stepped stilly and stel to his bedde,
Kest vp þe cortyn and creped withinne,
And set hir ful softly on þe bed-syde,
And lenged þere selly longe to loke quen he wakened.
Þe lede lay lurked a ful longe quyle,                          1195
Compast in his concience to quat þat cace my3t
Meue oþer amount—to meruayle hym po3t,
Bot 3et he sayde in hymself, 'More semly hit were
To aspye wyth my spelle in space quat ho wolde.'
Þen he wakenede, and wroth, and to hir warde torned,          1200
And vnlouked his y3e-lyddez, and let as hym wondered,
And sayned hym, as bi his sa3e þe sauer to worthe,
              with hande.
        Wyth chynne and cheke ful swete,
        Boþe quit and red in blande,                          1205
        Ful lufly con ho lete
        Wyth lyppez smal la3ande.

God moroun, Sir Gawayn,' sayde þat gay lady,
'3e ar a sleper vnsly3e, þat mon may slyde hider;
Now ar 3e tan as-tyt! Bot true vus may schape,              1210
I schal bynde yow in your bedde, þat be 3e trayst':

Under a bright coverlet with curtains around him,
And as he slumbered softly it seemed to him he heard
A small sound at his door, and suddenly it opened
And he heaves up his head out of the bedclothes,
He lifts up a corner of the curtain a little
And peers out cautiously to see what it might be.
It was the lady, the loveliest one to look at,
Who shut the door behind her without making a sound
And turned toward the bed, and the knight was embarrassed
And lay back to look as though he were asleep,
And with hushed steps she stole to his bed,
Lifted the curtain and crept inside
And softly set herself down on the bedside
And stayed there a long time watching for him to wake.
The knight went on pretending for a while
Turning over in his mind what this visitation
Might mean or lead to, and wondering at it.      *very honorable*
Yet he said to himself, "It would be better
To speak directly and ask what she wants.")
Then he woke, and stretched, and turned until he faced her
And opened his eyes wide as though he were startled,
And crossed himself as though to fend off temptation
                    with his hand.
            Her chin and her cheek were lovely,
            White and red mingling;
            Her way and her words were pretty
            And her small lips laughing.


"Good morning, Sir Gawain," said the beautiful lady,
"You are a careless sleeper if one can steal up on you.
Now you are caught just like that! But we can come to terms.
I will keep you captive in your bed, you can be sure of that."

'Al la3ande þe lady lanced þo bourdez.
'Goud moroun, gay,' quoþ Gawayn þe blyþe,
'Me schal worþe at your wille, and þat me wel lykez,
For I 3elde me 3ederly, and 3e3e after grace,       1215
And þat is þe best, be my dome, for me byhouez nede':
And þus he bourded a3ayn with mony a blyþe la3ter.
'Bot wolde 3e, lady louely, þen leue me grante,
And deprece your prysoun, and pray hym to ryse,
I wolde bo3e of þis bed, and busk me better;       1220
I schulde keuer þe more comfort to karp yow wyth.'
'Nay for soþe, beau sir,' sayd þat swete,
'3e schal not rise of your bedde, I rych yow better,
I schal happe yow here þat oþer half als,
And syþen karp wyth my kny3t þat I ka3t haue;       1225
For I wene wel, iwysse, Sir Wowen 3e are,
Þat alle þe worlde worchipez quere-so 3e ride;
Your honour, your hendelayk is hendely praysed
With lordez, wyth ladyes, with alle þat lyf bere.
And now 3e ar here, iwysse, and we bot oure one;       1230
My lorde and his ledez ar on lenþe faren,
Oþer burnez in her bedde, and my burdez als,
Þe dor drawen and dit with a derf haspe;
And syþen I haue in þis hous hym þat al lykez,
I schal ware my whyle wel, quyl hit lastez,       1235
      with tale.
        3e ar welcum to my cors,
        Yowre awen won to wale,
        Me behouez of fyne force
        Your seruaunt be, and schale.'       1240

'In god fayth,' quoþ Gawayn, 'gayn hit me þynkkez,
Þa3 I be not now he þat 3e of speken;

The lady laughed as she made light of it.
"Good morning, fair lady," Gawain said merrily.
"You will have your way with me, and I like the thought of that,
And I surrender immediately and beg for mercy,
And that, I believe, is the best I can do."
And thus he too made light of it and laughed about it.
"But, beautiful lady, if you would allow me,
If you were to release your prisoner and tell him to rise,
I would leave this bed and dress myself better,
And feel more at ease for talking with you."
"No indeed, fair sir," said that lovely lady.
"You shall not rise from your bed, for I have better plans.
I shall hold you tight on that other side too
And then converse with my knight when I have caught him.
For I am aware that you are Sir Gawain,
Whom all the world worships wherever you ride.
Your honor, your courtesy are endlessly praised
Among lords and ladies and all who are alive.
And now you are here, in truth, and we are alone.
My lord and his men are riding far from here.
The others are in their beds, and my ladies too;
The door shut and locked with a heavy bolt,
And since I have in this house the one whom they all like,
I shall use my time well as long as it lasts,

> and my talk.
>> You are welcome to my body
>> For your own sweet will.
>> I cannot help but be
>> Your servant, and so I will."

"In good faith," Gawain said, "fortune seems to have found me,
Though I am hardly the person you tell of.

To reche to such reuerence as ȝe reherce here  
I am wyȝe vnworþy, I wot wel myseluen.  
Bi God, I were glad, and yow god þoȝt,       1245  
At saȝe oþer at seruyce þat I sette myȝt  
To þe plesaunce of your prys—hit were a pure ioye.'  
'In god fayth, Sir Gawayn,' quoþ þe gay lady,  
'Þe prys and þe prowes þat plesez al oþer,  
If I hit lakked oþer set at lyȝt, hit were littel daynté;    1250  
Bot hit ar ladyes innoȝe þat leuer wer nowþe  
Haf þe, hende, in hor holde, as I þe habbe here,  
To daly with derely your daynté wordez,  
Keuer hem comfort and colen her carez,  
Þen much of þe garysoun oþer golde þat þay hauen.    1255  
Bot I louue þat ilk lorde þat þe lyfte haldez,  
I haf hit holly in my honde þat al desyres,  
     þurȝe grace.'  
    Scho made hym so gret chere,  
    Þat watz so fayr of face,  
    Þe knyȝt with speches skere       1261  
    Answared to vche a cace.  

'Madame,' quoþ þe myry mon, 'Mary yow ȝelde,  
For I haf founden, in god fayth, yowre fraunchis nobele,  
And oþer ful much of oþer folk fongen bi hor dedez,    1265  
Bot þe daynté þat þay delen, for my disert nys euen,  
Hit is þe worchyp of yourself, þat noȝt bot wel connez.'  
'Bi Mary,' quoþ þe menskful, 'me þynk hit an oþer;  
For were I worth al þe wone of wymmen alyue,  
And al þe wele of þe worlde were in my honde,     1270  
And I schulde chepen and chose to cheue me a lorde,  
For þe costes þat I haf knowen vpon þe, knyȝt, here,  
Of bewté and debonerté and blyþe semblaunt,

I am all unworthy, as I know myself,
To presume to the honor you ascribe to me.
I would be glad, by God, if it suited you
For me to offer some word or deed
To please your fair self. That would be pure joy."
"In good faith, Sir Gawain," said the lovely lady,
"If I belittled or slighted the honor and prowess
The rest of the world likes, that would not be right.
But there are many ladies who would be happy now
To hold you, good sir, as I hold you here,
And converse happily in courtly love talk.
It would give them more pleasure and deeper comfort
Than all of the treasure and gold that they have.
But I praise that one lord who reigns in heaven
That I have wholly in my hand what they all want,
                 through His grace."
          So pretty her ways are,
          And so lovely her face,
          Yet the knight's words are pure
          Whatever she says.


"Madam," said that merry man, "Mary reward you,
For your generosity, in good faith, seems noble to me.
There are some whose deeds earn honor from others,
But I do not deserve the esteem they accord me.
It is honor of your own that makes you speak well of me."
"By Mary," the lady said, "I see it another way.
For if I were worth all the women alive together,
And all the wealth of the world were in my hand
And I were to bargain and choose to have me a lord,
Because of the virtues, Knight, that I have known in you here,
Your fine looks and manners and spirited style,

And þat I haf er herkkened and halde hit here trwee,  
Þer schulde no freke vpon folde bifore yow be chosen.'     1275
'Iwysse, worþy,' quoþ þe wyȝe, 'ȝe haf waled wel better,
Bot I am proude of þe prys þat ȝe put on me,
And, soberly your seruaunt, my souerayn I holde yow,
And yowre knyȝt I becom, and Kryst yow forȝelde.'
Þus þay meled of muchquat til mydmorn paste,     1280
And ay þe lady let lyk as hym loued mych;
Þe freke ferde with defence, and feted ful fayre—
'Þaȝ I were burde bryȝtest', þe burde in mynde hade.
Þe lasse luf in his lode for lur þat he soȝt
         boute hone,     1285
    Þe dunte þat schulde hym deue,
    And nedez hit most be done.
    Þe lady þenn spek of leue,
    He granted hir ful sone.

Þenne ho gef hym god day, and wyth a glent laȝed,     1290
And as ho stod, ho stonyed hym wyth ful stor wordez:
'Now he þat spedez vche spech þis disport ȝelde yow!
Bot þat ȝe be Gawan, hit gotz in mynde.'
'Querfore?' quoþ þe freke, and freschly he askez,
Ferde lest he hade fayled in fourme of his castes;     1295
Bot þe burde hym blessed, and 'Bi þis skyl' sayde:
'So god as Gawayn gaynly is halden,
And cortaysye is closed so clene in hymseluen,
Couth not lyȝtly haf lenged so long wyth a lady,
Bot he had craued a cosse, bi his courtaysye,     1300
Bi sum towch of summe tryfle at sum talez ende.'
Þen quoþ Wowen: 'Iwysse, worþe as yow lykez;
I schal kysse at your comaundement, as a knyȝt fallez,

Which I had long heard about and now know to be true,
There is no knight on earth whom I would have chosen before you."
"Indeed, noble lady, you made a better choice,
But I am proud of the honor you place upon me;
I count myself your servant, certainly, and you my sovereign.
I have become your knight, and may Christ reward you."
They went on talking of this and that until past mid-morning
And all that time the lady let him know how much she loved him.
The knight fended her off, behaving correctly.
"Though I were the loveliest of all ladies," said the lady to herself,
"He carries no love with him"—with his fate looming
                    before him,
        The blow that would fell him,
        As things were bound to be.
        The lady said she would leave him.
        He accepted promptly.


Then she wished him good day, with a laughing glance,
And as she stood up she startled him with the sting in her words:
"Now may He who blesses each word reward you for this pleasure,
But I wonder whether you are Gawain after all."
"Why is that?" the knight asked as soon as she said it,
Fearing that he might have failed to speak with full courtesy,
But the lady blessed him and answered like this:
"Refined as they say Gawain's manners are,
With such chivalry as he is said to embody,
He could scarcely have stayed so long with a lady
Without asking for a kiss, if only from politeness,
At some point or pause, somewhere in the conversation."
Then Gawain said, "Indeed, whatever you will.
I shall kiss at your command, as a knight should,

And fire, lest he displese yow, so plede hit no more.'
Ho comes nerre with þat, and cachez hym in armez,　　　　1305
Loutez luflych adoun and þe leude kyssez.
Þay comly bykennen to Kryst ayþer oþer;
Ho dos hir forth at þe dore withouten dyn more;
And he ryches hym to ryse and rapes hym sone,
Clepes, to his chamberlayn, choses his wede,　　　　1310
Boȝez forth, quen he watz boun, blyþely to masse;
And þenne he meued to his mete þat menskly hym keped,
And made myry al day, til þe mone rysed,
　　　　　with game.
　　　　　　Watz neuer freke fayrer fonge　　　　1315
　　　　　　Bitwene two so dyngne dame,
　　　　　　Þe alder and þe ȝonge;
　　　　　　Much solace set þay same.


And ay þe lorde of þe londe is lent on his gamnez,
To hunt in holtez and heþe at hyndez barayne;　　　　1320
Such a sowme he þer slowe bi þat þe sunne heldet,
Of dos and of oþer dere, to deme were wonder.
Þenne fersly þay flokked in folk at þe laste,
And quykly of þe quelled dere a querré þay maked.
Þe best boȝed þerto with burnez innoghe,　　　　1325
Gedered þe grattest of gres þat þer were,
And didden hem derely vndo as þe dede askez;
Serched hem at þe asay summe þat þer were,
Two fyngeres þay fonde of þe fowlest of alle.
Syþen þay slyt þe slot, sesed þe erber,　　　　1330
Schaued wyth a scharp knyf, and þe schyre knitten;
Syþen rytte þay þe foure lymmes, and rent of þe hyde,
Þen brek þay þe balé, þe bowelez out token

Rather than displease you, so plead it no further."
At that she comes close to him and takes him in her arms,
Bends down tenderly and kisses the knight.
Politely they commend each other to Christ.
She goes out the door without another sound
And he makes ready to rise without more delay,
Calls for his chamberlain, chooses what to wear,
Sets out to Mass in high spirits as soon as he is dressed.
And then he went to his meal and put his mind to that
And amused himself all day in games until
           the moon rose.
      No knight ever was entertained better,
      Between two such fine ladies,
      The elder and the younger
      Kept him entertained with their graces.

And still the lord of the land is off hunting,
Chasing the childless hinds in woods and on heaths.
By the time the sun was setting he had killed so many
Does and other deer that they could hardly count them.
Then they rushed in, crowding together at the finish,
And soon assembled the slain deer into a single heap,
The highest lords went there with many men,
Picked out the fattest ones from the others
And had them cut up carefully in the correct way,
While some went on sorting out the ones that were left.
They found fat two fingers thick on the poorest of them.
Then they slit open the throat, seized the first stomach,
Sliced it out with a sharp knife and tied it shut.
Next they lopped the four limbs and flayed off the hide,
Broke open the belly and took out the bowels,

Lystily for laucyng þe lere of þe knot;
Þay gryped to þe gargulun, and grayþely departed          1335
Þe wesaunt fro þe wynt-hole, and walt out þe guttez;
Þen scher þay out þe schulderez with her scharp knyuez,
Haled hem by a lyttel hole to haue hole sydes.
Siþen britned þay þe brest and brayden hit in twynne,
And eft at þe gargulun bigynez on þenne,                  1340
Ryuez hit vp radly ry3t to þe by3t,
Voydez out þe avanters, and verayly þerafter
Alle þe rymez by þe rybbez radly þay lance;
So ryde þay of by resoun bi þe rygge bonez,
Euenden to þe haunche, þat henged alle samen,            1345
And heuen hit vp al hole, and hwen hit of þere,
And þat þay neme for þe noumbles bi nome, as I trowe,
          bi kynde;
            Bi þe by3t al of þe þy3es
            Þe lappez þay lance bihynde;                   1350
            To hewe hit in two þay hy3es,
            Bi þe bakbon to vnbynde.

Boþe þe hede and þe hals þay hwen of þenne,
And syþen sunder þay þe sydez swyft fro þe chyne,
And þe corbeles fee þay kest in a greue;                 1355
Þenn þurled þay ayþer þik side þur3 bi þe rybbe,
And henged þenne ayþer bi ho3ez of þe fourchez,
Vche freke for his fee, as fallez for to haue.
Vpon a felle of þe fayre best fede þay þayr houndes
Wyth þe lyuer and þe ly3tez, þe leþer of þe paunchez,     1360
And bred baþed in blod blende þeramongez.
Baldely þay blw prys, bayed þayr rachchez,
Syþen fonge þay her flesche, folden to home,

Quickly casting them aside, saving the knots of flesh.
They grasped the throat and sundered with one stroke
The gullet from the windpipe, and flung out the guts.
Then they sliced the shoulders with their sharp knives,
Hauled the sinews through a little hole to keep the sides whole.
Then they split the breast and pried it apart
And then went back to the gullet again.
They severed it swiftly right to the fork,
Emptied out the entrails, and then truly
They cut all the membranes along the ribs skillfully,
Clearing them away along the bones of the back,
All the way to the haunch that hung from it whole,
And they hauled it up in one piece and cut out those bits
Inside that are eaten, known as the numbles,
            to my knowledge,
        Near the fork of the thighs,
        Cutting behind folds of skin.
        They hew it in two pieces
        To split the backbone.

Both the head and the neck they hew off then,
And next they quickly sever the sides from the chine
And they toss the crows' fee into a thicket.
And then they pierced through both sides along the ribs
And hung them both up by the hocks of the legs,
Each man taking the fee that by right was his.
On one of the finest skins they fed their hounds,
The liver and the lights, the tripe of the paunches,
And bread bathed in blood mixed in with it all.
Loudly they blew the horn and the hounds bayed.
Then they took their meat, each of them, and headed for home,

Strakande ful stoutly mony stif motez.
Bi þat þe dayly3t watz done þe douthe watz al wonen          1365
Into þe comly castel, þer þe kny3t bidez
       ful stille,
     Wyth blys and bry3t fyr bette.
     Þe lorde is comen þertylle;
     When Gawayn wyth hym mette          1370
     Þer watz bot wele at wylle.


Thenne comaunded þe lorde in þat sale to samen alle þe meny,
Boþe þe ladyes on loghe to ly3t with her burdes
Bifore alle þe folk on þe flette, frekez he beddez
Verayly his venysoun to fech hym byforne,          1375
And al godly in gomen Gawayn he called,
Techez hym to þe tayles of ful tayt bestes,
Schewez hym þe schyree grece schorne vpon rybbes.
'How payez yow þis play? Haf I prys wonnen?
Haue I þryuandely þonk þur3 my craft serued?'          1380
'3e iwysse,' quoþ þat oþer wy3e, 'here is wayth fayrest
Þat I se3 þis seuen 3ere in sesoun of wynter.'
'And al I gif yow, Gawayn,' quoþ þe gome þenne,
'For by acorde of couenaunt 3e craue hit as your awen.'
'Þis is soth,' quoþ þe segge, 'I say yow þat ilke:          1385
Þat I haf worthyly wonnen þis wonez wythinne,
Iwysse with as god wylle hit worþez to 3ourez.'
He hasppez his fayre hals his armez wythinne,
And kysses hym as comlyly as he couþe awyse:
''Tas yow þere my cheuicaunce, I cheued no more;          1390
I wowche hit saf fynly, þa3 feler hit were.'
'Hit is god,' quoþ þe godmon, 'grant mercy þerfore.
Hit may be such hit is þe better, and 3e me breue wolde
Where 3e wan þis ilk wele bi wytte of yorseluen.'

Sounding the horns loudly again and again.
By the time the daylight was done, all the company
Had come into the great castle, where the knight was quietly
        waiting.
        There were high hearts and bright fires burning
        As the lord came home
        And Gawain was coming
        To meet him, and great joy between them.


Then the lord summoned all of them to gather in that hall,
And the ladies to come down too, bringing their maidens with them.
Before the entire assembly there he has his men
Bring his share of the venison before him,
And in the best of humor he called to Gawain
To show him the tally of the swift deer.
He points out the fine flesh carved from the ribs.
"What do you think of this game? Have I won your approval?
Do I deserve your full thanks for the way I have hunted?"
"Indeed," said the other, "here is the finest take
That I have seen, these seven years, in the winter season."
"And I give it all to you, Gawain," the lord said then.
"By the terms of our covenant you may claim it as your own."
"True enough," the knight said, "and I say the same to you:
What I have won honorably here in the house,
And with as good a will, I am sure, shall be made yours."
And he takes his fine neck between his arms    *LMAO*
And kisses him as gracefully as he can.
"There you have my winnings, for I gained nothing else.
I wish I had something greater to give you."
"It is good," the good man said, "and I thank you for it.
It might even be the better of the two if you told me
Where it was that your own merits won you this prize."

'Þat watz not forward,' quoþ he, 'frayst me no more.　　　　1395
For ȝe haf tan þat yow tydez, trawe non oþer
　　　　ȝe mowe.'
　　　　Þay laȝed, and made hem blyþe
　　　　Wyth lotez þat were to lowe;
　　　　To soper þay ȝede as-swyþe,　　　　1400
　　　　Wyth dayntés nwe innowe.


And syþen by þe chymné in chamber þay seten,
Wyȝez þe walle wyn weȝed to hem oft,
And efte in her bourdyng þay bayþen in þe morn
To fylle þe same forwardez þat þay byfore maden:　　　　1405
Wat chaunce so bytydez hor cheuysaunce to chaunge,
What nwez so þay nome, at naȝt quen þay metten.
Þay acorded of þe couenauntez byfore þe court alle;
Þe beuerage watz broȝt forth in bourde at þat tyme,
Þenne þay louelych leȝten leue at þe last,　　　　1410
Vche burne to his bedde busked bylyue.
Bi þat þe coke hade crowen and cakled bot þryse,
Þe lorde watz lopen of his bedde, þe leudez vchone;
So þat þe mete and þe masse watz metely delyuered,
Þe douthe dressed to þe wod, er any day sprenged,　　　　1415
　　　　to chace;
　　　　Heȝ with hunte and hornez
　　　　Þurȝ playnez þay passe in space,
　　　　Vncoupled among þo þornez
　　　　Rachez þat ran on race.　　　　1420


Sone þay calle of a quest in a ker syde,
Þe hunt rehayted þe houndez þat hit fyrst mynged,
Wylde wordez hym warp wyth a wrast noyce;
Þe howndez þat hit herde hastid þider swyþe,

"That was not part of the pact," he said, "ask me no more.
For you have been paid what was owed you, and should want
        nothing besides."
      They laughed and made light of it
      With wit and wisdom.
      Then they went in to eat
      The fine supper ready for them.

And afterwards, when they sat in the chamber by the fire,
And the servants kept bringing them choice wines,
They agreed, in their banter, again and again, that the next day
They would keep to the agreement they had made before
And exchange whatever gains fortune might grant them,
However novel those might be, when they met at nighttime.
They confirmed their covenant before the whole court.
The drink was brought, and they drank to it, laughing.
Then at last they bade each other a courteous good night
And each of them went at once to his bed.
By the time the cock had crowed and cackled three times
The lord had leapt from his bed, and each of the knights,
So that the meal and the Mass were served promptly,
And the whole company off to the wood before daylight,
       to the hunt.
      Loud with the sound of horns
      They sweep over the plain,
      Unleash the hounds among the thorns
      And let them run.

They pick up a scent before long at the edge of a marsh.
The hunt urged on the hounds that found it first,
Calling wild words to them at the top of their voices.
The hounds that heard it raced to the spot,

And fellen as fast to þe fuyt, fourty at ones; 1425
Þenne such a glauer ande glam of gedered rachchez
Ros, þat þe rocherez rungen aboute;
Hunterez hem hardened with horne and wyth muthe.
Þen al in a semblé sweyed togeder,
Bitwene a flosche in þat fryth and a foo cragge; 1430
In a knot bi a clyffe, at þe kerre syde,
Þer as þe rogh rocher vnrydely watz fallen,
Þay ferden to þe fyndyng, and frekez hem after;
Þay vmbekesten þe knarre and þe knot boþe,
Wyȝez, whyl þay wysten wel wythinne hem hit were, 1435
Þe best þat þer breued watz wyth þe blodhoundez.
Þenne þay beten on þe buskez, and bede hym vpryse,
And he vnsoundyly out soȝt seggez ouerþwert;
On þe sellokest swyn swenged out þere,
Long sythen fro þe sounder þat siȝed for olde, 1440
For he watz breme, bor alþer-grattest,
Ful grymme quen he gronyed; þenne greued mony,
For þre at þe fyrst þrast he þryȝt to þe erþe,
And sparred forth good sped boute spyt more.
Þise oþer halowed hyghe! ful hyȝe, and hay! hay! cryed, 1445
Haden hornez to mouþe, heterly rechated;
Mony watz þe myry mouthe of men and of houndez
Þat buskkez after þis bor with bost and wyth noyse
                to quelle.
            Ful oft he bydez þe baye, 1450
            And maymez þe mute inn melle;
            He hurtez of þe houndez, and þay
            Ful ȝomerly ȝaule and ȝelle.

Schalkez to schote at hym schowen to þenne,
Haled to hym of her arewez, hitten hym oft; 1455

Rushing in to take up the trail, forty at once.
Then such a ruckus and racket of crowding hounds
Rose that the rocks around them rang with it,
The hunters urging them on with horns and shouts.
Then all of them rushed together into a single pack
Between a pool in the forest and a towering crag.
In a pile of rocks by a cliff, at the marsh side,
There where the rough boulders had tumbled together,
They raced to flush the game, and the knights after them.
They cast about in the stone heaps and the rocky hill,
All of them sure of what was hiding inside there,
The beast that the bloodhounds announced with their baying.
They beat on the bushes and shouted to rouse him,
And he burst out in a fury, heading straight for the men,
A boar of monstrous size, suddenly sprung,
One who had long been the ancient of swine,
For he was a fierce pig, bigger than the rest,
His grunt ferocious, striking fear into many.
Three of them he threw to the ground with his first rush
And dashed off at full speed without doing more damage.
The others shouted "Hi! Hi!" and "Hay! Hay!" they called,
With their horns to their mouths, loud in the chase.
Many were the merry sounds of men and of hounds
Running with noise and high voices after this boar
       for the kill.
      Often he turns at bay
      And maims those that press closely.
      He hurts the hounds and they
      Howl and shriek piteously.

Then those prepared to shoot at him pushed forward,
Aimed their arrows at him, hit him again and again,

Bot þe poyntez payred at þe pyth þat pyȝt in his scheldez,
And þe barbez of his browe bite non wolde—
Þaȝ þe schauen schaft schyndered in pecez,
Þe hede hypped aȝayn were-so-euer hit hitte.
Bot quen þe dyntez hym dered of her dryȝe strokez,      1460
Þen, braynwod for bate, on burnez he rasez,
Hurtez hem ful heterly þer he forth hyȝez,
And mony arȝed þerat, and on lyte droȝen.
Bot þe lorde on a lyȝt horce launces hym after,
As burne bolde vpon bent his bugle he blowez,      1465
He rechated, and rode þurȝ ronez ful þyk,
Suande þis wylde swyn til þe sunne schafted.
Þis day wyth þis ilk dede þay dryuen on þis wyse,
Whyle oure luflych lede lys in his bedde,
Gawayn grayþely at home, in gerez ful ryche      1470
       of hewe.
         Þe lady noȝt forȝate,
         Com to hym to salue;
         Ful erly ho watz hym ate
         His mode for to remwe.      1475


Ho commes to þe cortyn, and at þe knyȝt totes.
Sir Wawen her welcumed worþy on fyrst,
And ho hym ȝeldez aȝayn ful ȝerne of hir wordez,
Settez hir softly by his syde, and swyþely ho laȝez,
And wyth a luflych loke ho layde hym þyse wordez:      1480
'Sir, ȝif ȝe be Wawen, wonder me þynkkez,
Wyȝe þat is so wel wrast alway to god,
And connez not of compaynye þe costez vndertake,
And if mon kennes yow hom to knowe, ȝe kest hom of your mynde;
Þou hatz forȝeten ȝederly þat ȝisterday I taȝtte      1485
Bi alder-truest token of talk þat I cowþe.'

But the points were turned by the tough shield of his hide,
And the barbs would not bite into his brow.
Instead, the smooth shafts were splintered into pieces.
The heads leapt away again wherever they hit.
But when the heat of their heavy blows began to tell upon him,
Then, in a frenzy to fight them, he rushes at the knights,
Wounding them suddenly as he hurled himself into them,
So that many of them panicked and scrambled aside.
But the lord dashes after him on a spirited horse.
Blowing his bugle as a bold knight in the chase,
He called them to follow him and rode through the thickets
In pursuit of this wild boar as long as the sun was shining.
So on that single chase they spent the whole of that day
While our fair knight Gawain is lying in bed
At home, at his ease, in sumptuous garments
       of bright colors.
     The lady did not fail to come
     To wish him good morning.
     Early indeed she was at him
     To waken his feeling.

She comes to the curtain and peeps at the knight.
Sir Gawain welcomes her politely, to start with,
And she can scarcely wait with her answers.
With a quick laugh she sits down softly beside him,
And these words she said to him, with a melting glance:
"I wonder, sir, whether you are really Gawain,
A knight so set upon doing the right thing,
But does not know how to behave politely
And pays no attention even if he is instructed.
You have already forgotten what I taught you yesterday
Though I expressed it to you as clearly as I could."

'What is þat?' quoþ þe wyghe, 'Iwysse I wot neuer;
If hit be sothe þat ȝe breue, þe blame is myn awen.'
'ȝet I kende yow of kyssyng,' quoþ þe clere þenne,
'Quere-so countenaunce is couþe quikly to clayme:　　　　　1490
Þat bicumes vche a knyȝt þat cortaysy vses.'
'Do way,' quoþ þat derf mon, 'my dere, þat speche,
For þat durst I not do, lest I deuayed were;
If I were werned, I were wrang, iwysse, ȝif I profered.'
'Ma fay,' quoþ þe meré wyf, 'ȝe may not be werned,　　　　　1495
ȝe ar stif innoghe to constrayne wyth strenkþe, ȝif yow lykez,
ȝif any were so vilanous þat yow devaye wolde.'
'ȝe, be God,' quoþ Gawayn, 'good is your speche,
Bot þrete is vnþryuande in þede þer I lende,
And vche gift þat is geuen not with goud wylle.　　　　　1500
I am at your comaundement, to kysse quen yow lykez,
ȝe may lach quen yow lyst, and leue quen yow þynkkez,
　　　　　in space.'
　　　　　Þe lady loutez adoun,
　　　　　And comlyly kysses his face,　　　　　1505
　　　　　Much speche þay þer expoun
　　　　　Of druryes greme and grace.


'I woled wyt at yow, wyȝe,' þat worþy þer sayde,
'And yow wrathed not þerwyth, what were þe skylle
Þat so ȝong and so ȝepe as ȝe at þis tyme,　　　　　1510
So cortayse, so knyȝtyly, as ȝe ar knowen oute—
And of alle cheualry to chose, þe chef þyng alosed
Is þe lel layk of luf, þe lettrure of armes;
For to telle of þis teuelyng of þis trwe knyȝtez,
Hit is þe tytelet token and tyxt of her werkkez,　　　　　1515
How ledes for her lele luf hor lyuez han auntered,
Endured for her drury dulful stoundez,

"Did you?" the knight asked. "I did not understand it.
If what you say is true, I am to blame."
"I gave you a lesson in kissing," the lady said.
"Where a favor is offered, it should be claimed promptly
By any knight who pretends to be courteous."
"My dear," that brave man said, "do not say such a thing.
I would not dare to risk your denying me.
If you were to refuse me I would be in the wrong."
"By my faith," she said merrily, "you could not be refused.
You are strong enough to have your own way, if you want to,
If anyone were so graceless as to refuse you."
"Indeed," Gawain said, "you put it plainly.
But force is frowned on in the country I come from,
And any gift not given with good will.

*woman respecter 8000*

I am at your command, to kiss when you please.
Take hold when you like, and when you are ready
      let go."
         The lady bends down
         And softly kisses his face.
         They talk for a long time then
         Of love's sorrow and happiness.


"I wish you would tell me, Knight," that lady said,
"Unless it annoys you, what reason there could be
Why someone as young and dashing as you are now,
And as courteous and knightly as you are known to be—
And in all of chivalry the thing that is most praised,
Along with the art of arms, is the true sport of love,
For the tales of how true knights have engaged in this venture
Are the testimony and text of their achievements,
Telling how some, for their true love, have risked their lives,
Enduring terrible trials because of them,

And after wenged with her walour and voyded her care,
And broȝt blysse into boure with bountees hor awen—
And ȝe ar knyȝt comlokest kyd of your elde,                          1520
Your worde and your worchip walkez ayquere,
And I haf seten by yourself here sere twyes,
Ȝet herde I neuer of your hed helde no wordez
Þat euer longed to luf, lasse ne more;
And ȝe, þat ar so cortays and coynt of your hetes,                   1525
Oghe to a ȝonke þynk ȝern to schewe
And teche sum tokenez of trweluf craftes.
Why! ar ȝe lewed, þat alle þe los weldez?
Oþer elles ȝe demen me to dille your dalyaunce to herken?
    For schame!                                                       1530
        I com hider sengel, and sitte
        To lerne at yow sum game;
        Dos, techez me of your wytte,
        Whil my lorde is fro hame.'


'In goud fayþe,' quoþ Gawayn, 'God yow forȝelde!                     1535
Gret is þe gode gle, and gomen to me huge,
Þat so worþy as ȝe wolde wynne hidere,
And pyne yow with so pouer a mon, as play wyth your knyȝt
With anyskynnez countenaunce, hit keuerez me ese;
Bot to take þe toruayle to myself to trwluf expoun,                  1540
And towche þe temez of tyxt and talez of armez
To yow þat, I wot wel, weldez more slyȝt
Of þat art, bi þe half, or a hundreth of seche
As I am, oþer euer schal, in erde þer I leue,
Hit were a folé felefolde, my fre, by my trawþe.                     1545
I wolde yowre wylnyng worche at my myȝt,
As I am hyȝly bihalden, and euermore wylle
Be seruaunt to yourseluen, so saue me Dryȝtyn!'

And were avenged by bravery at last and put their pains behind them
And by their own courage brought joy to their ladies' bowers—
And you are famous as the most courtly knight of your time,
Your renown and glory have gone everywhere,
Have let me sit here beside you a second time
And never have I heard a word from your mouth
That might be the language of love, or anything like it.
And you who are so courtly, with such winning ways,
Ought to offer a little instruction to a young thing
And teach her some token of the art of true love.
Do you know nothing, for all your fame?
Or do you think me too dull for your language of love?

      Shame on you!
    I come here alone and sit
    To learn the art from you.
    Now while my lord is out
    Please teach me what you know."


"In good faith," Gawain said, "God reward you!
What a joy, and what great pleasure to me
To have someone so noble pay me a visit
And take such pains with so humble a fellow, entertaining
Your knight with such favors—what a comfort to me!
But to take upon myself the task of expounding true love,
Repeating the terms of the text and the tales of adventures
To you who know half again as much of these matters
Or a hundred times more, I am sure, than I do
Or ever will as long as I live in the world,
Would be foolish in more ways than I can say, my lady.
I will do whatever I can to please you,
As I am bound to, and I will remain
Your faithful servant, so may God save me!"

*Handwritten margin note:* interesting how back home he's the least recognized of the round table, but out here where he's The Greatest he still doesn't accept it

Pus hym frayned þat fre, and fondet hym ofte,
For to haf wonnen hym to woȝe, what-so scho poȝt ellex;
Bot he defended hym so fayr þat no faut semed,
Ne non euel on nawþer halue, nawþer þay wysten
   bot blysse.
    Þay laȝed and layked longe;
    At þe last scho con hym kysse,    1555
    Hir leue fayre con scho fonge
    And went hir waye, iwysse.

Then ruþes hym þe renk and ryses to þe masse,
And siþen hor diner watz dyȝt and derely serued.
Þe lede with þe ladyez layked alle day,    1560
Bot þe lorde ouer þe londez launced ful ofte,
Swez his vncely swyn, þat swyngez bi þe bonkkez
And bote þe best of his brachez þe bakkez in sunder
Þer he bode in his bay, tel bawemen hit breken,
And madee hym mawgref his hed for to mwe vtter,    1565
So felle flonez þer flete when þe folk gedered.
Bot ȝet þe styffest to start bi stoundez he made,
Til at þe last he watz so mat he myȝt no more renne,
Bot in þe hast þat he myȝt he to a hole wynnez
Of a rasse bi a rokk þer rennez þe boerne.    1570
He gete þe bonk at his bak, bigynez to scrape,
Þe froþe femed at his mouth vnfayre bi þe wykez,
Whettez his whyte tuschez; with hym þen irked
Alle þe burnez so bolde þat hym by stoden
To nye hym on-ferum, bot neȝe hym non durst    1575
   for woþe;
    He hade hurt so mony byforne
    Þat al þuȝt þenne ful loþe

So she put him to the test and tried many times
To woo him into wrongdoing, whatever else she had in mind.
But he defended himself so well that nothing seemed wrong
On either side, and there appeared to be nothing between them
        but bliss.
      They stayed long laughing and playing,
      And at last she gave him a kiss
      As a graceful leavetaking,
      And went her way, with this.


Then the knight rouses himself and goes off to Mass
And then his dinner was laid and splendidly served.
All day the knight was entertained by the ladies
While the lord galloped back and forth over the countryside
After this fierce boar that raced up the steep hillsides,
And bit the best of his dogs, breaking their backs in two.
There he stood at bay until the archers dislodged him
For all his defiance, and made him move on again.
Then many arrows flew as the crowd closed in.
Yet again and again he made the bravest give ground
Until at last he was too tired to run any longer,
But he moves as fast as he can to get to a hollow
On a bank by a rock with a brook running beside it.
He gets the bank at his back and starts pawing the ground.
Froth foamed from his mouth, ugly at the corners.
He whets his white tusks. By then all the knights
Who had been so bold to get close to him were not so eager.
They kept their distance and dared not go near him,
        Too deadly.
      He had hurt so many already
      That none of them wanted

Be more wyth his tusches torne,
Þat breme watz and braynwod bothe,　　　　　　1580

Til þe knyȝt com hymself, kachande his blonk,
Syȝ hym byde at þe bay, his burnez bysyde;
He lyȝtes luflych adoun, leuez his corsour,
Braydez out a bryȝt bront and bigly forth strydez,
Foundez fast þurȝ þe forth þer þe felle bydez.
Þe wylde watz war of þe wyȝe with weppen in honde,
Hef hyȝly þe here, so hetterly he fnast
Þat fele ferde for þe freke, lest felle hym þe worre.
Þe swyn settez hym out on þe segge euen,
Þat þe burne and þe bor were boþe vpon hepez　　　1590
In þe wyȝtest of þe water; þe worre hade þat oþer,
For þe mon merkkez hym wel, as þay mette fyrst,
Set sadly þe scharp in þe slot euen,
Hit hym vp to þe hult, þat þe hert schyndered,
And he ȝarrande hym ȝelde, and ȝedoun þe water　　1595
　　　ful tyt.
　　　A hundreth houndez hym hent,
　　　Þat bremely con hym bite,
　　　Burnez him broȝt to bent,
　　　And doggez to dethe endite.　　　　　　　1600

There watz blawyng of prys in mony breme horne,
Heȝe halowing on hiȝe with haþelez þat myȝt;
Brachetes bayed þat best, as bidden þe maysterez
Of þat chargeaunt chace þat were chef huntes.
Þenne a wyȝe þat watz wys vpon wodcraftez　　　1605
To vnlace þis bor lufly bigynnez.
Fyrst he hewes of his hed and on hiȝe settez,
And syþen rendez him al roghe bi þe rygge after,

To be torn by his tusks when he
Was enraged and driven mad.

Until the knight of the castle himself comes, spurring his horse,
Sees him standing at bay with the men around him.
Lightly he leaps to the ground, leaving his mount.
He draws a bright sword and strides forward, undaunted,
Splashing ahead through the stream to where the wild beast is waiting.
The creature saw the man with the weapon in his hand.
Every bristle stood straight up and he snorted so fiercely
That the others were afraid the knight would have the worst of it.
The boar makes a rush straight at the man
And he and the knight came crashing together
Where the water ran wildest, and the beast came out worst,
For the man struck him hard as they first met,
Ran the sharp blade straight in above the breastbone,
Stabbing up to the hilt, cutting clear through the heart,
And he buckled snarling and collapsed in the water
        all at once.
      A hundred hounds seized him
      In their sharp jaws.
      And the men dragged him
      Ashore for the dogs to finish.

Then many loud horns were blaring that he was down,
And the men all shouting at the tops of their voices,
The hounds baying their best at their masters' bidding
Who had led the hunt on that terrible chase.
Then a knight who knew how to live in the forest
Began to butcher the boar the right way.
First he hews off his head and sets it up high,
Then roughly rends him clear to the backbone,

Braydez out þe boweles, brennez hom on glede,
With bred blent þerwith his braches rewardez.                    1610
Syþen he britnez out þe brawen in bryȝt brode cheldez,
And hatz out þe hastlettez, as hiȝtly bisemez;
And ȝet hem halchez al hole þe haluez togeder,
And syþen on a stif stange stoutly hem henges.
Now with þis ilk swyn þay swengen to home;                    1615
Þe bores hed watz borne bifore þe burnes seluen
Þat him forferde in þe forþe þurȝ forse of his honde
            so stronge.
            Til he seȝ Sir Gawayne
            In halle hym þoȝt ful longe;                    1620
            He calde, and he com gayn
            His feez þer for to fonge.

Þe lorde ful lowde with lote and laȝter myry,
When he seȝe Sir Gawayn, with solace he spekez;
Þe goude ladyez were geten, and gedered þe meyny,            1625
He schewez hem þe scheldez, and schapes hem þe tale
Of þe largesse and þe lenþe, þe liþernez alse
Of þe were of þe wylde swyn in wod þer he fled.
Þat oþer knyȝt ful comly comended his dedez,
And praysed hit as gret prys þat he proued hade,            1630
For suche a brawne of a best, þe bolde burne sayde,
Ne such sydes of a swyn segh he neuer are.
Þenne hondeled þay þe hoge hed, þe hende mon hit praysed,
And let lodly þerat þe lorde for to here.
'Now, Gawayn,' quoþ þe godmon, 'þis gomen is your awen        1635
Bi fyn forwarde and faste, faythely ȝe knowe.'
'Hit is sothe,' quoþ þe segge, 'and as siker trwe
Alle my get I schal yow gif agayn, bi my trawþe.'
He hent þe haþel aboute þe halse, and hendely hym kysses,

Pulls out the bowels and broils them on the coals,
Blends them with bread and rewards the dogs with them.
Then he cuts out the flesh in bright, broad slabs
And carefully lifts out the innards that are for eating,
Then he binds the two halves back together again,
And hangs the whole thing up securely on a heavy pole,
And with this pig they have taken they start toward home,
Holding up the boar's head in front of the hunter
Who had killed him in the water with the strength
      of his arm,
        To whom it seems a long time
        Until he sees, in the hall, Sir Gawain
        Coming when he calls him
        To collect what he may be given.


The lord's voice was loud and he laughed merrily
When he saw Sir Gawain, and his words were happy.
The fair ladies were sent for, and all the others.
He shows them the boar's flesh and tells them its story:
The size and length, and the fierceness besides
Of the wild pig in the woods wanting to escape them.
That other knight gracefully commended his hunting,
Praising the great courage he had displayed.
Such a mound of boar's meat, the bold knight said,
And such sides of wild pig he had never seen.
Then they handled the huge head and the courtly knight praised it
And told the lord how terrifying it looked.
"Now, Gawain," the good man said, "this kill is your own
By promise and covenant, as of course you know."
"As you say," the knight said, "and you have my word
That I shall give you all I have taken, upon my honor."
He embraced the knight around the neck and kissed him courteously

And eftersones of þe same he serued hym þere.                                      1640
'Now ar we euen,' quoþ þe haþel, 'in þis euentide
Of alle þe couenauntes þat we knyt, syþen I com hider,
       bi lawe.'
      Þe lorde sayde, 'Bi saynt Gile,
      Ʒe ar þe best þat I knowe!                            1645
      Ʒe ben ryche in a whyle,
      Such chaffer and ȝe drowe.'


Þenne þay teldet tablez trestes alofte,
Kesten cloþez vpon; clere lyȝt þenne
Wakned bi woȝez, waxen torches;                                                    1650
Seggez sette and serued in sale al aboute;
Much glam and gle glent vp þerinne
Aboute þe fyre vpon flet, and on fele wyse
At þe soper and after, mony aþel songez,
As coundutes of Krystmasse and carolez newe                                        1655
With al þe manerly merþe þat mon may of telle,
And euer oure luflych knyȝt þe lady bisyde.
Such semblaunt to þat segge semly ho made
Wyth stille stollen countenaunce, þat stalworth to plese,
Þat al forwondered watz þe wyȝe, and wroth with hymseluen,   1660
Bot he nolde not for his nuture nurne hir aȝaynez,
Bot dalt with hir al in daynté, how-se-euer þe dede turned
      towrast.
      Quen þay hade played in halle
      As longe as hor wylle hom last,                      1665
      To chambre he con hym calle,
      And to þe chemné þay past.


Ande þer þay dronken, and dalten, and demed eft nwe
To norne on þe same note on Nwe ȝerez euen;

And then served him the same way a second time.
"Now for this evening," the knight said, "we are even,
And all the pledges that I made since I came here are paid
      in full."
    The lord said, "By Saint Giles
    You are the best I know.
    You will be rich in a while
    If all your dealings turn out so."

Then they set up the trestles and the tables across them,
Cast cloths over them, and then they brought light,
Kindling the wax torches along the walls.
They sat and were served all down the hall,
Much merriment and laughter rippling in the room
Around the fire on the hearth, with entertainments
During supper and after, many lively songs,
Descants for Christmas, new carols among them,
All the finest amusements a man may tell of.
And all the while our courtly knight sat next to the lady.
So enticing were all her expressions toward him,
With glances stolen sidelong to attract that brave man,
That he was embarrassed, and annoyed with himself,
But his manners kept him from returning her courtship,
Yet he tried to answer politely, however she
      turned it.
    When for all in the great room
    The entertainments were over
    The lord told the knight to come
    And they went to his chimney corner.

And there they drank and laughed, and decided to play
Their game to the same tune on New Year's Eve.

Bot þe knyȝt craued leue to kayre on þe morn,      1670
For hit watz neȝ at þe terme þat he to schulde.
Þe lorde hym letted of þat, to lenge hym resteyed,
And sayde, 'As I am trwe segge, I siker my trawþe
Þou schal cheue to þe grene chapel þy charres to make,
Leude, on Nw ȝerez lyȝt, longe bifore pryme.      1675
Forþy þow lye in þy loft and lach þyn ese,
And I schal hunt in þis holt, and halde þe towchez,
Chaunge wyth þe cheuisaunce, bi þat I charre hider;
For I haf fraysted þe twys, and faythful I fynde þe.
Now "þrid tyme þrowe best" þenk on þe morne,      1680
Make we mery quyl we may and mynne vpon joye,
For þe lur may mon lach when-so mon lykez.'
Þis watz grayþely graunted, and Gawayn is lenged,
Bliþe broȝt watz hym drynk, and þay to bedde ȝeden
         with liȝt.      1685
      Sir Gawayn lis and slepes
      Ful stille and softe al niȝt;
      Þe lorde þat his craftez kepes,
      Ful erly he watz diȝt.


After messe a morsel he and his men token;      1690
Miry watz þe mornyng, his mounture he askes.
Alle þe haþeles þat on horse schulde helden hym after
Were boun busked on hor blonkkez bifore þe halle ȝatez.
Ferly fayre watz þe folde, for þe forst clenged;
In rede rudede vpon rak rises þe sunne,      1695
And ful clere costez þe clowdes of þe welkyn.
Hunteres vnhardeled bi a holt syde,
Rocheres roungen bi rys for rurde of her hornes;
Summe fel in þe fute þer þe fox bade,
Traylez ofte a traueres bi traunt of her wyles;      1700

But the knight asked leave to ride out in the morning,
For the time was near when he had sworn to go.
The lord brushed that aside and urged him to linger,
Saying, "On my faith as a knight, I give you my word
You will reach the Green Chapel, for your errand there
On New Year's dawn, Prince, long before prime.
So lie in your high room and take your ease
And I shall hunt in these woods and keep our agreement
And exchange the winnings with you, whatever I bring back,
For I have tested you twice and found you of good faith.
Now tomorrow remember, 'the third throw pays for all.'
Let us be merry while we may, and have joy in our minds,
For sorrow can catch us whenever it pleases."
So Gawain agreed at once that he would stay.
They drank on it gladly, and then the lights led them
       to bed.
     Sir Gawain lies sleeping
     Soundly and still all night.
     The lord, with plans turning
     In mind, was dressed before daylight.

After Mass, he and his men have a morsel.
The morning was clear. He asks for his horse.
All the mounted knights who would ride after him
Were ready, on their horses, before the hall gates.
The earth was a splendor, with the clinging frost.
The red sun rises flaming upon the drifts of mist
And sails past the clouds of the sky in its full radiance.
Hunters unleashed the hounds at the edge of a wood.
The rocks among the trees rang with the sound of their hooves.
Some picked up the trail of the fox and followed it,
The track weaving this way and that on a cunning course.

A kenet kryes þerof, þe hunt on hym calles;
His felaȝes fallen hym to, þat fnasted ful þike,
Runnen forth in a rabel in his ryȝt fare,
And he fyskez hem byfore; þay founden hym sone,
And quen þay seghe hym with syȝt þay sued hym fast,    1705
Wreȝande hym ful weterly with a wroth noyse;
And he trantes and tornayeez þurȝ mony tene greue,
Hauilounez, and herkenez bi heggez ful ofte.
At þe last bi a littel dich he lepez ouer a spenne,
Stelez out ful stilly bi a strothe rande,    1710
Went haf wylt of þe wode with wylez fro þe houndes;
Þenne watz he went, er he wyst, to a wale tryster,
Þer þre þro at a þrich þrat hym at ones,
      al graye.
    He blenched aȝayn bilyue    1715
    And stifly start on-stray,
    With alle þe wo on lyue
    To þe wod he went away.

Thenne watz ht list vpon lif to lyþen þe houndez,
When alle þe mute hade hym met, menged togeder:    1720
Suche a sorȝe at þat syȝt þay sette on his hede
As alle þe clamberande clyffes hade clatered on hepes;
Here he watz halawed, when haþelez hym metten,
Loude he watz ȝayned with ȝarande speche;
Þer he watz þreted and ofte þef called,    1725
And ay þe titleres at his tayl, þat tary he ne myȝt;
Ofte he watz runnen at, when he out rayked,
And ofte reled in aȝayn, so Reniarde watz wylé.
And ȝe he lad hem bi lagmon, þe lorde and his meyny,
On þis maner bi þe mountes quyle myd-ouer-vnder,    1730
Whyle þe hende knyȝt at home holsumly slepes

[ 116 ]

A small hound keeps up the cry and the hunt answers him.
His fellows follow him, sniffing the scent,
Running ahead in a pack along the right track,
And he races ahead. They found him before long
And when they caught sight of him they spurred on the chase,
Shouting at him loudly with angry cries,
And he dodges and doubles back through the dense thickets,
Often turning in his tracks, to hear them from the hedges.
At last by a little ditch he leaps over a thorn brake,
Slips out secretly by a line of bushes,
Thought he had given the hounds the slip with his tricks,
When he found himself face to face with a hunting station
Where three fierce dogs rushed at him all at once,

        all gray.
    He dodged out of their way
    And off at a full run;
    With all the woe he could carry
    To the woods he was gone.


Then how the heart leapt to hear the hounds
When the whole pack had met and mingled together.
Such calamities they called down upon his head
As would have brought all the crowding cliffs clattering down in heaps.
Here they hallooed after him, when the hunters spied him,
And they greeted him shouting bad names after him.
There he was threatened and called "Thief! Thief!"
With the hounds always at his tail keeping him on the run.
Often they rushed at him when he made for the open,
And often spun back again, for Reynard was wily,
And oh, he led them a long dance, the lord and his company,
Over the mountains, like this, as the sun climbed to midday,
While the courtly knight is still sleeping soundly at home

Withinne þe comly cortynes, on þe colde morne.
Bot þe lady for luf let not to slepe,
Ne þe purpose to payre þat py3t in hir hert,
Bot ros hir vp radly, rayked hir þeder                                  1735
In a mery mantyle, mete to þe erþe,
Þat watz furred ful fyne with fellez wel pured,
No hwez goud on hir hede bot þe ha3er stones
Trased aboute hir tressour be twenty in clusteres;
Hir þryuen face and hir þrote þrowen al naked,                           1740
Hir brest bare bifore, and bihinde eke.
Ho comez withinne þe chambre dore, and closes hit hir after,
Wayuez vp a wyndow, and on þe wy3e callez,
And radly þus rehayted hym with hir riche wordes,
            with chere:                                                  1745
        'A! mon, how may þou slepe,
        Þis morning is so clere?'
        He watz in drowping depe,
        Bot þenne he con hir here.


In dre3 droupyng of dreme draueled þat noble,                            1750
As mon þat watz in mornyng of mony þro þo3tes,
How þat destiné schulde þat day dele hym his wyrde
At þe grene chapel, when he þe gome metes,
And bihoues his buffet abide withoute debate more;
Bot quen þat comly com he keuered his wyttes,                            1755
Swenges out of þe sweuenes, and swarez with hast.
Þe lady luflych com la3ande swete,
Felle ouer his fayre face, and fetly hym kyssed;
He welcumez hir worþily with a wale chere.
He se3 hir so glorious and gayly atyred,                                 1760
So fautles of hir fetures and of so fyne hewes,

Inside the elegant curtains, through the cold morning.
But love would not allow the lady to sleep
Nor let go of the purpose pinned into her heart,
But she was up early and on her way there
In an elegant mantle that reached to the ground,
A splendor of furs and pelts artfully trimmed,
Nothing adorning her head but the glittering jewels
In clusters of twenty, in a fillet over her hair,
Her lovely face and all of her throat naked.
Her breast was bare, and her back also.
She comes in through the bedroom door and shuts it behind her,
Opens a window and calls to the knight,
Rousing him right there with her pretty speech,
    teasing him:
        "Ah, man, how can you sleep
        With the morning so fair?"
        Though his slumber was deep,
        Through it he heard her.

That noble knight murmured from the dark depths of his dreams
As a man held down by many heavy thoughts
Of that day when destiny was to deal his fate to him
At the Green Chapel, when he would meet the knight there
And have to lie still for his stroke without defending himself.
But when that beautiful creature comes he recovers his wits,
Breaks out of his dreams and responds at once.
Laughing tenderly, the lovely lady
Bent over his fine face and gave him a sweet kiss.
He welcomed her warmly, happy to have her there.
So glorious she looked, her garments so fine,
Her features so flawless, her skin so fair,

Wi3t wallande joye warmed his hert.
With smoþe smylyng and smolt þay smeten into merþe,
Þat al watz blis and bonchef þat breke hem bitwene,
         and wynne.               1765
      Þay lanced wordes gode,
      Much wele þen watz þerinne;
      Gret perile bitwene hem stod,
      Nif Maré of hir kny3t mynne.

For þat prynces of pris depresed hym so þikke,     1770
Nurned hym so ne3e þe þred, þat nede hym bihoued
Oþer lach þer hir luf, oþer lodly refuse.
He cared for his cortaysye, lest craþayn he were,
And more for his meschef 3if he schulde make synne,
And be traytor to þat tolke þat þat telde a3t.       1775
'God schylde,' quoþ þe schalk, 'þat schal not befalle!'
With luf-la3yng a lyt he layd hym bysyde
Alle þe spechez of specialté þat sprange of her mouthe.
Quoþ þat burde to þe burne, 'Blame 3e disserue,
3if 3e luf not þat lyf þat 3e lye nexte,        1780
Bifore alle þe wy3ez in þe worlde wounded in hert,
Bot if 3e haf a lemman, a leuer, þat yow lykez better,
And folden fayth to þat fre, festned so harde
Þat yow lausen ne lyst—and þat I leue nouþe;
And þat 3e telle me þat now trwly I pray yow,    1785
For alle þe lufez vpon lyue layne not þe soþe
        for gile.'
      Þe kny3t sayde, 'Be sayn Jon,'
      And smeþely con he smyle,
      'In fayth I welde ri3t non,        1790
      Ne non wil welde þe quile.'

That joy welled up in him and warmed his heart.
Gently, with fond smiles, they dally in pleasure,
Complete bliss and happiness breaking forth between them,
        and joy.
      The sweet words flew between them,
      Charged with delight.
      Great danger lurked between them,
      Should Mary forget her knight.


For that sumptuous princess pressed him so hard,
Lured him so near to the edge that he knew he must
Either give in to her love or rudely refuse it.
He was concerned for his courtesy, not wanting to be coarse,
And still more for the damage it would do if he sinned
And betrayed the lord in whose house he was staying.
"God save me," he said, "that will not happen."
Lightly, with kind laughter, he turned aside
All the seductive talk that leapt from her mouth.
The lady said to the knight, "It is wrong of you
Not to love the one you are lying next to,
Whose heart is more hurt than any in the world,
But if you have another love, one dearer, whom you love more
And have given your word to that lady in good faith
And would not want to break it—that is what I believe.
Tell me the truth about it now, I beg you.
In the name of all the loves in the world, do not hide the truth
        to be cunning."
      The knight said, "By Saint John,"
      With a gentle smile,
      "Lover have I none,
      Nor will have for a while."

'Þat is a worde,' quoþ þat wyȝt, 'þat worst is of alle,
Bot I am swared for soþe, þat sore me þinkkez.
Kysse me now comly, and I schal cach heþen,
I may bot mourne vpon molde, as may þat much louyes.'　　1795
Sykande ho sweȝe doun and semly hym kyssed,
And siþen ho seueres hym fro, and says as ho stondes,
'Now, dere, at þis departyng do me þis ese,
Gif me sumquat of þy gifte, þi gloue if hit were,
Þat I may mynne on þe, mon, my mournyng to lassen.'　　1800
'Now iwysse,' quoþ þat wyȝe, 'I wolde I hade here
Þe leuest þing for þy luf þat I in londe welde,
For ȝe haf deserued, for soþe, sellyly ofte
More rewarde bi resoun þen I reche myȝt;
Bot to dele yow for drurye þat dawed bot neked,　　1805
Hit is not your honour to haf at þis tyme
A gloue for a garysoun of Gawaynez giftez,
And I am here an erande in erdez vncouþe,
And haue no men wyth no malez with menskful þingez;
Þat mislykez me, ladé, for luf at þis tyme,　　1810
Iche tolke mon do as he is tan, tas to non ille
　　　　　ne pine.'
　　　　'Nay, hende of hyȝe honours,'
　　　　Quoþ þat lufsum vnder lyne,
　　　　'Þaȝ I hade noȝt of yourez,　　1815
　　　　Ȝet schulde ȝe haue of myne.'


Ho raȝt hym a riche rynk of red golde werkez,
Wyth a starande ston stondande alofte
Þat bere blusschande bemez as þe bryȝt sunne;
Wyt ȝe wel, hit watz worth wele ful hoge.　　1820
Bot þe renk hit renayed, and redyly he sayde,
'I wil no giftez, for Gode, my gay, at þis tyme;

"That is the worst thing," she said, "that you could have told me.
But I have had my answer and it is hard to bear.
Now kiss me kindly and I shall be on my way
To the sorrowing life of a woman lost to love."
With a sigh she bent down and kissed him tenderly,
And then she lets go of him and says as she stands there,
"Now, my love, as I leave you, do me one kindness.
Give me some token of you, your glove or some such thing,
To remember you by and comfort me in my longing."
"Now truly," the man said, "I wish I had here
Whatever thing I prize most, to give you for your love,
For you have surely deserved, many times over,
More than anything I might have given you.
But a token of love would not amount to much.
It would afford you no honor, now, to have
A glove to treasure, as a gift from Gawain,
And I am here on an errand in an unknown land
And have no porters with packs full of precious things,
Which I regret at this moment, lady, because of your love.
Each man can do only so much, and it is no use
   complaining."
   "No, most honored knight,"
   Said she of the fair body,
   "Though I have nothing from you yet,
   You should have something from me."

She held out to him a handsome ring wrought of red gold
With a shining stone standing up out of it,
Its radiant beams like the bright sun.
You can be sure it was worth a great fortune.
But the knight refused it at once, saying,
"Before God, lady, I want no gifts at this time.

I haf none yow to norne, ne noȝt wyl I take.'
Ho bede hit hym ful bysily, and he hir bode wernes,
And swere swyfte by his sothe þat he hit sese nolde,                    1825
And ho soré þat he forsoke, and sayde þerafter,
'If ȝe renay my rynk, to ryche for hit semez,
Ȝe wolde not so hyȝly halden be to me,
I schal gif yow my girdel, þat gaynes yow lasse.'
Ho laȝt a lace lyȝtly þat leke vmbe hir sydez,                         1830
Knit vpon hir kyrtel vnder þe clere mantyle,
Gered hit watz with grene sylke and with golde schaped,
Noȝt bot arounde brayden, beten with fyngrez;
And þat ho bede to þe burne, and blyþely bisoȝt,
Þaȝ hit vnworþi were, þat he hit take wolde.                           1835
And he nay þat he nolde neghe in no wyse
Nauþer golde ne garysoun, er God hym grace sende
To acheue to þe chaunce þat he hade chosen þere.
'And þerfore, I pray yow, displese yow noȝt,
And lettez be your bisinesse, for I bayþe hit yow neuer                1840
        to graunte;
            I am derely to yow biholde
            Bicause of your sembelaunt,
            And euer in hot and colde
            To be your trwe seruaunt.'                                 1845


'Now forsake ȝe þis silke,' sayde þe burde þenne,
'For hit is symple in hitself? And so hit wel semez.
Lo! so hit is littel, and lasse hit is worþy;
Bot who-so knew þe costes þat knit ar þerinne,
He wolde hit prayse at more prys, parauenture;                        1850
For quat gome so is gorde with þis grene lace,
While he hit hade hemely halched aboute,
Þer is no haþel vnder heuen tohewe hym þat myȝt,

I have none to offer you and I will take none."
She pressed him further but he would not accept it,
Swearing upon his honor that he would not have it.
And she was sad that he refused it, and finally said,
"If you will not take my ring because it seems too costly
And you do not want to be so deeply indebted to me,
I will give you my belt, which may not seem so precious to you."
With a flick she undid a knot fastened at her waist,
Tied around her tunic under the bright mantle.
It was covered with green silk and embroidered with gold
All around the edges, and with gold fringes,
And with all her graces she offered that to the knight,
Urging him to take it, unworthy though it was,
But he insisted that he would not, for any reason,
Accept gold or gift until God had given him
The grace to achieve the mission he had followed that far.
"And therefore I beg you not to be offended
But give up your offers, for I can never

        accept them.

        I am deeply indebted to you
        For the graces you have shown me,
        And will be a true servant to you
        Whatever season it may be."


"Do you refuse this silk now," the lady said then,
"Because it seems such a slight thing, in itself?
It is true, it is little, and does not look like much,
But anyone who knew the powers bound up in it
Perhaps would hold it in higher esteem.
For if a man has this green belt fastened around him,
As long as it is knotted about his waist
There is no knight under heaven who can cut him down,

For he my3t not be slayn for sly3t vpon erþe.'

Þen kest þe kny3t, and hit come to his hert                    1855

Hit were a juel for þe jopardé þat hym iugged were:

When he acheued to þe chapel his chek for to fech,

My3t he haf slypped to be vnslayn, þe sle3t were noble.

Þenne he þulged with hir þrepe and þoled hir to speke,

And ho bere on hym þe belt and bede hit hym swyþe—          1860

And he granted and hym gafe with a goud wylle—

And biso3t hym, for hir sake, disceuer hit neuer,

Bot to lelly layne fro hir lorde; þe leude hym acordez

Þat neuer wy3e schulde hit wyt, iwysse, bot þay twayne

        for no3te;                                   1865

     He þonkked hir oft ful swyþe,

     Ful þro with hert and þo3t.

     Bi þat on þrynne syþe

     Ho hatz kyst þe kny3t so to3t.

Thenne lachchez ho hir leue, and leuez hym þere,            1870

For more myrþe of þat mon mo3t ho not gete.

When ho watz gon, Sir Gawayn gerez hym sone,

Rises and riches hym in araye noble,

Lays vp þe luf-lace þe lady hym ra3t,

Hid hit ful holdely, þer he hit eft fonde.                 1875

Syþen cheuely to þe chapel choses he þe waye,

Preuély aproched to a prest, and prayed hym þere

Þat he wolde lyste his lyf and lern hym better

How his sawle schulde be saued when he schuld seye heþen.

Þere he schrof hym schyrly and schewed his mysdedez,       1880

Of þe more and þe mynne, and merci besechez,

And of absolucioun he on þe segge calles;

And he asoyled hym surely and sette hym so clene

As domezday schulde haf ben di3t on þe morn.

And there is no cunning on earth that can kill him."
This made the knight reflect, and went to his heart.
It would be a jewel for the jeopardy just ahead of him
When he arrived at the Green Chapel to be dealt his fate.
If it could keep him from being killed, it was a noble device.
Then he waited to hear what else she might say to him
And she pled with him to take the belt, urging it upon him
Until he accepted it, and she was glad to give it
And begged him for her sake to keep it secret,
And never let her lord learn of it, and the knight agreed
That no one should know of it, indeed, but the two of them,
       whatever might happen.
        He thanked her warmly
        With all his heart and thought.
        And then three times she
        Kissed that brave knight.

Then she turns from him and leaves him there
Since she would have no more pleasure with that man.
When she was gone, Gawain puts on his garments.
He gets up and arrays himself in noble attire,
Hides away the love-belt the lady had given him,
Carefully concealing it where he would find it later.
Then at once he made his way to the chapel,
Went to a priest privately and begged him there
To lift up his life and teach him to be better
So that his soul would be saved when he saw heaven.
There he confessed completely and said what his sins were,
The great and the small, and pled for mercy,
Calling upon the priest to grant him absolution,
And the priest absolved him altogether so he would be clean
Though the next dawn revealed the day of judgment.

And syþen he mace hym as mery among þe fre ladyes,    1885
With comlych caroles and alle kynnes ioye,
As neuer he did bot þat daye, to þe derk ny3t,
      with blys.
        Vche mon hade daynté þare
        Of hym, and sayde, 'Iwysse,    1890
        Þus myry he watz neuer are,
        Syn he com hider, er þis.'

Now hym lenge in þat lee, þer luf hym bityde!
3et is þe lorde on þe launde ledande his gomnes.
He hatz forfaren þis fox þat he fol3ed longe;    1895
As he sprent ouer a spenne to spye þe schrewe,
Þer as he herd þe howndes þat hasted hym swyþe,
Renaud com richchande þur3 a ro3e greue,
And alle þe rabel in a res ry3t at his helez.
Þe wy3e watz war of þe wylde, and warly abides,    1900
And braydez out þe bry3t bronde, and at þe best castez.
And he schunt for þe scharp, and schulde haf arered;
A rach rapes hym to, ry3t er he my3t,
And ry3t bifore þe hors fete þay fel on hym alle,
And woried me þis wyly wyth a wroth noyse.    1905
Þe lorde ly3tez bilyue, and lachez hym sone,
Rased hym ful radly out of þe rach mouþes,
Haldez he3e ouer his hede, halowez faste,
And þer bayen hym mony braþ houndez.
Huntes hy3ed hem þeder with hornez ful mony,    1910
Ay rechatande ary3t til þay þe renk se3en.
Bi þat watz comen his compeyny noble,
Alle þat euer ber bugle blowed at ones,
And alle þise oþer halowed þat hade no hornes;

Then he joined the amusements among the court ladies
With graceful dances and pleasures of all kinds,
And more than any day he had known, until the dark night,
        he was happy.
        And he raised everyone's
        Spirits so that they said
        They had not seen him, since
        He came there, in such a merry mood.


Now let him linger in that haven, and love be with him!
While the lord is still out in the field leading his men.
He has killed this fox that he followed for so long.
As he leapt over a thorn hedge, looking for the villain,
Hearing the hounds that were hard on his heels,
Reynard comes dashing out of a dense thicket
And all the rabble in a rush behind him.
The lord saw the wild creature and waited and was ready
And he draws the bright sword and slashes at the beast,
Who shies at the stroke and tries to turn back,
But a hound is before him and heads him off.
And right before the horse's hooves they all fell on him
With a roar of rage, mauling that cunning creature.
The lord leaps to the ground and seizes him,
Snatches him right up out of the hounds' mouths,
Holds him high over his head with a loud shout
Above all the hounds baying at him in fury.
The hunters rushed toward him, all sounding their horns,
Rallying the rest until they caught sight of him.
Then when that noble company was assembled,
All who had bugles blew them at once,
And the others all shouted, who had no horns.

Hit watz þe myriest mute þat euer men herde,                                  1915
Þe rich rurd þat þer watz raysed for Renaude saule
       with lote.
       Hor houndez þay þer rewarde,
       Her hedez þay fawne and frote,
       And syþen þay tan Reynarde,                                 1920
       And tyruen of his cote.

And þenne þay helden to home, for hit watz nieȝ nyȝt,
Strakande ful stoutly in hor store hornez.
Þe lorde is lyȝt at þe laste at hys lef home,
Fyndez fire vpon flet, þe freke þer-byside,                                    1925
Sir Gawayn þe gode, þat glad watz withalle,
Among þe ladies for luf he ladde much ioye;
He were a bleaunt of blwe þat bradde to þe erþe,
His surkot semed hym wel þat softe watz forred,
And his hode of þat ilke henged on his schulder,                              1930
Blande al of blaunner were boþe al aboute.
He metez me þis godmon inmyddez þe flore,
And al with gomen he hym gret, and goudly he sayde,
'I schal fylle vpon fyrst oure forwardez nouþe,
Þat we spedly han spoken, þer spared watz no drynk.'
Þen acoles he þe knyȝt and kysses hym þryes,                                  1936
As sauerly and sadly as he hem sette couþe.
'Bi Kryst,' quoþ þat oþer knyȝt, 'ȝe cach much sele
In cheuisaunce of þis chaffer, ȝif ȝe hade goud chepez.'
'Ȝe, of þe chepe no charg,' quoþ chefly þat oþer,                             1940
'As is pertly payed þe chepez þat I aȝte.'
'Mary,' quoþ þat oþer mon, 'myn is bihynde,
For I haf hunted al þis day, and noȝt haf I geten
Bot þis foule fox felle—þe fende haf þe godez!—

It was the merriest uproar that ever man heard,
The resounding din they raised, the racket for
      Reynard's soul.
     They give the hounds their reward,
     Pet them and praise them,
     And then they take Reynard
     And strip his coat from him.


And then they start home, for it is nearly night,
Blowing loudly on their horns as they go.
The lord alights at last, happy to be home
With a fire in the hall and the knight waiting beside it,
The good Sir Gawain, who was in high spirits
Among the ladies, and their loving entertainments.
He was wearing a rich blue mantle that reached to the ground.
His outer cloak lined with soft fur suited him perfectly,
And his hood which was like it hung over his shoulders,
Both trimmed all around with borders of white fur.
He meets this good man in the middle of the floor
And greets him and the others, and says to him, smiling,
"I shall begin by fulfilling our agreement
That we sealed, to suit us both, when the drink was not spared,"
Then he embraces the knight and kisses him three times
As sweetly and earnestly as he could manage.
"By Christ," said the other knight, "you have done well
In the prize you have taken, if the price was right."
"Never mind the price," the other said,
"As long as I paid the earnings I owed."
"Mary," the other man said, "mine is far short of yours,
For I have hunted all day and taken nothing
But this foul fox pelt—the devil take it!—

And þat is ful pore for to pay for suche prys þinges 1945
As ȝe haf þryȝt me here þro, suche þre cosses
     so gode.'
      'Inoȝ,' quoþ Sir Gawayn,
      'I þonk yow, bi þe rode',
      And how þe fox watz slayn 1950
      He tolde hym as þay stode.


With merþe and mynstralsye, wyth metez at hor wylle,
Þay maden as mery as any men moȝten—
With laȝyng of ladies, with lotez of bordes
Gawayn and þe godemon so glad were þay boþe— 1955
Bot if þe douthe had doted, oþer dronken ben oþer.
Boþe þe mon and þe meyny maden mony iapez,
Til þe sesoun watz seȝen þat þay seuer moste;
Burnez to hor bedde behoued at þe laste.
Þenne loȝly his leue at þe lorde fyrst 1960
Fochchez þis fre mon, and fayre he hym þonkkez:
'Of such a selly soiorne as I haf hade here,
Your honour at þis hyȝe fest, þe hyȝe fest, þ hyȝe yow ȝelde!
I ȝef yow me for on of yourez, if yowreself lykez,
For I mot nedes, as ȝe wot, meue to-morne, 1965
And ȝe me take sum tolke to teche, as ȝe hyȝt,
Þe gate to þe grene chapel, as God wyl me suffer
To dele on Nw Ȝerez day þe dome of my wyrdes.'
'In god fayþe,' quoþ þe godmon, 'wyth a goud wylle
Al þat euer I yow hyȝt halde schal I redé.' 1970
Þer asyngnes he a seruaunt to sett hym in þe waye,
And coundue hym by þe downez, þat he no drechch had,
For to ferk þurȝ þe fryth and fare at þe gaynest
     bi greue.

Which is pitiful repayment for such precious things
As you have pressed on me so warmly here, three such
       good kisses."
      "Enough," said Sir Gawain,
      "I thank you, by the Rood."
      And how the fox was slain
      He told him, there as they stood.


With amusements and minstrelsy and as much as they could eat
They celebrated as merrily as ever men might—
Unless they were dunces or hopelessly drunk—
With the laughter of ladies, and turns of wit.
Gawain and the good man were both in high humor.
The knight and all of them joined in the merrymaking
Until it was time for them to separate,
And for all of them to be off to their own beds.
Then this noble knight humbly takes his leave, first,
Of the lord there, thanking him gracefully,
"For the lavish visit that I have had here
And your courtesy at this high feast, may the high king reward you.
I offer myself as one of your own, if that would please you,
But as you know, I must be gone by tomorrow,
And I ask you for a knight to show me, as you promised,
The way to the Green Chapel, so that God may let me
Fulfill my fate there on New Year's Day."
"In good faith," the good man said, "with a good will,
All that ever I promised you I will have ready."
At that he assigns a servant to put him on the path
And lead him over the hills so that he would have no trouble
Riding in the woods and finding the right way
      through the thickets.

Þe lorde Gawayn con þonk,                    1975
Such worchip he wolde hym weue.
Þen at þo ladyez wlonk
Þe kny3t hatz tan his leue.

With care and wyth kyssyng he carppez hem tille,
And fele þryuande þonkkez he þrat hom to haue,     1980
And þay 3elden hym a3ayn 3eply þat ilk;
Þay bikende hym to Kryst with ful colde sykyngez.
Syþen fro þe meyny he menskly departes;
Vche mon þat he mette, he made hem a þonke
For his seruyse and his solace and his sere pyne,     1985
Þat þay wyth busynes had been aboute hym to serue;
And vche segge as soré to seuer with hym þere
As þay hade wonde worþyly with þat wlonk euer.
Þen with ledes and ly3t he watz ladde to his chambre
And blyþely bro3t to his bedde to be at his rest.     1990
3if he ne slepe soundyly say ne dar I,
For he hade muche on þe morn to mynne, 3if he wolde,
          in þo3t.
     Let hym ly3e þere stille,
     He hatz nere þat he so3t;              1995
     And 3e wyl a whyle be stylle
     I schal telle yow how þay wro3t.

For all the kindness he had been shown
The lord Gawain thanks and honors him.
He turns to the ladies then
And takes his leave of them.

They went on talking sadly, and kissing,
And he expressed his thanks to each one of them,
And they replied to him in the same vein.
Sighing with grief, they commended him to Christ.
Then gracefully he takes his leave of that company,
Thanking each of them once more as he came to him
For his service and kindness and each trouble he had taken,
For they had all gone to great lengths to care for him,
And each was as stricken there at parting with him
As though they had lived with that lord loyally all their lives.
Then he was led to his bedchamber by boys holding lights,
And brought happily to his bed to be at rest.
I cannot say whether he slept soundly,
For there was much about the morning that he might have had
        on his mind.
       Let him lie there still
       So close to what he came for.
       If you listen for a while
       I will tell you what they did later.

# IV

Now neȝez þe Nw ȝere, and þe nyȝt passez,
Þe day dryuez to þe derk, as Dryȝtyn biddez;
Bot wylde wederez of þe worlde wakned þeroute,                    2000
Clowdes kesten kenly þe colde to þe erþe,
Wyth nyȝe innoghe of þe norþe, þe naked to tene;
Þe snawe snitered ful snart, þat snayped þe wylde;
Þe werbelande wynde wapped fro þe hyȝe,
And drof vche dale ful of dryftes ful grete.                     2005
Þe leude lystened ful wel þat leȝ in his bedde,
Þaȝ he lowkez his liddez, ful lyttel he slepes;
Bi vch kok þat crue he knwe wel þe steuen.
Deliuerly he dressed vp, er þe day sprenged,
For þere watz lyȝt of a laumpe þat lemed in his chambre;         2010
He called to his chamberlayn, þat cofly hym swared,
And bede hym bryng hym his bruny and his blonk sadel;
Þat oþer ferkez hym vp and fechez hym his wedez,
And grayþez me Sir Gawayn vpon a grett wyse.
Fyrst he clad hym in his cloþez þe colde for to were,           2015
And syþen his oþer harnays, þat holdely watz keped,
Boþe his paunce and his platez, piked ful clene,
Þe ryngez rokked of þe roust of his riche bruny;
And al watz fresch as vpon fyrst, and he watz fayn þenne
          to þonk;                                              2020
          He hade vpon vche pece,
          Wypped ful wel and wlonk;

# IV

Now the New Year comes near and the night passes.
At heaven's command the day presses hard on the darkness.
The wild weather of the world wakens outside,
Clouds casting fierce cold across the earth
With bitter blasts from the north to lash the naked.
The snow shivered down, freezing, stinging the wild creatures,
The shrieking wind came bursting out of the sky
And piled up high drifts in all the hollows.
The knight listens to it all, lying in his bed.
Though his eyelids are shut he barely sleeps.
Each time the cock crows he recalls what awaits him.
He got up quickly before the day began,
By the light of a lamp left burning in his bedchamber.
He called to his bedservant, who appeared before him,
And told him to bring his coat of mail and saddle his horse.
The man is brisk and brings him his clothes and his armor
And gets Gawain ready in full splendor.
First he put his clothes on him to ward off the cold
And then the rest of his armor that had been well taken care of.
His body armor and each plate were brightly burnished,
The rust rubbed off the rings of his rich coat of mail,
And all was as clean as when it was new, and for this    *methodically*
        he was grateful.    *prepares*
        He puts on each piece,
        Well polished and lustrous.

Þe gayest into Grece,
Þe burne bede bryng his blonk.

Whyle þe wlonkest wedes he warp on hymseluen—                2025
His cote wyth þe conysaunce of þe clere werkez
Ennurned vpon veluet, vertuus stonez
Aboute beten and bounden, enbrauded semez,
And fayre furred withinne wyth fayre pelures—
Ȝet laft he not þe lace, þe ladiez gifte,                2030
Þat forgat not Gawayn for gode of hymseluen.
Bi he hade belted þe bronde vpon his balȝe haunchez,
Þenn dressed he his drurye double hym aboute,
Swyþe sweþled vmbe his swange swetely þat knyȝt
Þe gordel of þe grene silke, þat gay wel bisemed,                2035
Vpon þat ryol red cloþe þat ryche watz to schewe.
Bot wered not þis ilk wyȝe for wele þis gordel,
For pryde of þe pendauntez, þaȝ polyst þay were,
And þaȝ þe glyterande golde glent vpon endez,
Bot for to sauen hymself, when suffer hym byhoued,                2040
To byde bale withoute dabate of bronde hym to were
        oþer knyffe.
            Bi þat þe bolde mon boun
            Wynnez þeroute bilyue,
            Alle þe meyny of renoun                2045
            He þonkkez ofte ful ryue.

Thenne watz Gryngolet grayþe, þat gret watz and huge,
And hade ben soiourned sauerly and in a siker wyse,
Hym lyst prik for poynt, þat proude hors þenne.
Þe wyȝe wynnez hym to and wytez on his lyre,                2050
And sayde soberly hymself and by his soth swerez:
'Here is a meyny in þis mote þat on menske þenkkez,

[ 138 ]

None finer from there to Greece.
He sends for his horse.

While he fastened on the finest pieces himself—
His tunic with its blazon in bright embroidery
Embellished upon velvet, with precious stones
Stitched and bound into it, and embroidered seams,
All artfully lined with the finest of furs—
He did not leave the belt behind, the lady's gift:
Gawain did not forget that, for his own good.
When he had buckled his sword over his hipbones
He drew the love token around him twice.
Quickly and with pleasure that knight bound his waist
In the girdle of green silk that became him well,
Standing out brightly against the rich red cloth.
But it was not for its worth that the knight wore that belt,
Nor the splendor of its pendants for all their flashing,
Though the glittering gold glinted at the ends of them,
But to save himself when his time came to suffer
And wait for death with no sword to defend him
          or other blade.
      After that, in full dress, the brave man
      Strides out briskly
      And thanks all those nobles again
      Abundantly.

Then Gryngolet was made ready, and a huge horse he was,
And he had been stabled and cared for in comfort,
And was in high fettle then, that proud steed.
The knight goes up to him and looks him over
And says to himself soberly, swearing on his honor,
"There are men within this moat whose minds are noble.

Þe mon hem maynteines, ioy mot þay haue;
Þe leue lady on lyue luf hir bityde;
ȝif þay for charyté cherysen a gest, 2055
And halden honour in her honde, þe haþel hem ȝelde
Þat haldez þe heuen vpon hyȝe, and also yow alle!
And ȝif I myȝt lyf vpon londe lede any quyle,
I schuld rech yow sum rewarde redyly, if I myȝt.'
Þenn steppez he into stirop and strydez alofte; 2060
His schalk schewed hym his schelde, on schulder he hit laȝt,
Gordez to Gryngolet with his gilt helez,
And he startez on þe ston, stod he no lenger
        to praunce.
      His haþel on hors watz þenne, 2065
      Þat bere his spere and launce.
      'Þis kastel to Kryst I kenne':
      He gef hit ay god chaunce.


The brygge watz brayde doun, and þe brode ȝatez
Vnbarred and born open vpon boþe halue. 2070
Þe burne blessed hym bilyue, and þe bredez passed—
Prayses þe porter bifore þe prynce kneled,
Gef hym God and goud day, þat Gawayn he saue—
And went on his way with his wyȝe one,
Þat schulde teche hym to tourne to þat tene place 2075
Þer þe ruful race he schulde resayue.
Þay boȝen bi bonkkez þer boȝez ar bare,
Þay clomben bi clyffez þer clengez þe colde.
Þe heuen watz vphalt, bot vgly þer-vnder;
Mist muged on þe mor, malt on þe mountez, 2080
Vch hille hade a hatte, a myst-hakel huge.
Brokez byled and breke bi bonkkez aboute,
Schyre schaterande on schorez, þer þay doun schowued.

May joy come to the man who maintains them.
And may love be with the most delightful lady on earth.
If they entertained a guest this way out of charity,
With their hands full of honors, may the Lord repay them
Who holds the heavens high, and also each one of you!
And if I were to live in this land any longer
I would find some way to reward you, if I could."
Then he puts his foot in the stirrup and mounts his horse.
His man gave him his shield and he slung it on his shoulder,
Gives Gryngolet a touch with his gilded heels,
And he sprang from the paving stones, not even staying
        to prance.
      The knight on his steed,
      Bearing his lance and spear,
      Said, "I wish this castle good fortune
      And leave it in Christ's care."

The drawbridge was lowered and the broad gates
Were unbarred and they swung open on both sides.
The knight crossed himself quickly and passed over the planks,
Praised the porter who knelt before the prince,
Praying, "God give him a good day and save Gawain,"
And he went on his way with his one man
Who was to show him the turnings to that woeful place
Where he was to receive the deadly stroke.
They wind along hillsides where the trees are bare,
They climb among cliffs where the ice clings.
Under the high heaven the clouds were threatening.
Mist drizzled on moors, sliding over the mountains.
Each hill had a hat, a huge cloak of cloud.
Brooks boiled and broke their banks about them
Foaming white at the sides and running down in rapids.

Wela wylle watz þe way þer þay bi wod schulden,
Til hit watz sone sesoun þat þe sunne ryses 2085
þat tyde.
Þay were on a hille ful hyȝe,
Þe quyte snaw lay bisyde;
Þe burne þat rod hym by
Bede his mayster abide. 2090

'For I haf wonnen yow hider, wyȝe, at þis tyme,
And now nar ȝe not fer fro þat note place
Þat ȝe han spied and spuryed so specially after;
Bot I schal say yow for soþe, syþen I yow knowe,
And ȝe ar a lede vpon lyue þat I wel louy, 2095
Wolde ȝe worch bi my wytte, ȝe worþed þe better.
Þe place þat ȝe prece to ful perelous is halden;
Þer wonez a wyȝe in þat waste, þe worst vpon erþe,
For he is stiffe and sturne, and to strike louies,
And more he is þen any mon vpon myddelerde, 2100
And his body bigger þen þe best fowre
Þat ar in Arþurez hous, Hestor, oþer oþer.
He cheuez þat chaunce at þe chapel grene,
Þer passes non bi þat place so proude in his armes
Þat he ne dyngez hym to deþe with dynt of his honde; 2105
For he is a mon methles, and mercy non vses,
For be hit chorle oþer chaplayn þat bi þe chapel rydes,
Monk oþer masseprest, oþer any mon elles,
Hym þynk as queme hym to quelle as quyk go hymseluen.
Forþy I say þe, as soþe as ȝe in sadel sitte, 2110
Com ȝe þere, ȝe be kylled, may þe knyȝt rede,
Trawe ȝe me þat trwely, þaȝ ȝe had twenty lyues
to spende.

The way through the forest was hard to follow
Until the moment had come for the sun to rise,
      that time.
    They were on a hill, and around them
    The white snow everywhere.
    The man who rode beside him
    Told his master to stop there.

"For I have brought you here, sir, at this time,
And now you are not far from the place we spoke of
That you have looked for and asked about with such concern.
But I will tell you the truth, since I know you
And there is no man alive whom I love more.
If you take my advice it will be better for you.
The place you are hurrying toward is known for its peril.
In that wilderness lives the worst creature in the world,
And he is strong and gruesome and eager for a fight,
And he is more huge than any man on Middle Earth
And his body is bigger than the best four
In Arthur's house, or Hector, or anyone anywhere.
He waits at the Green Chapel for what comes his way.
No one passes by that place, however proud in his arms,
Whom he does not strike dead with a blow of his hand.
For he is a wild monster with no use for mercy,
And whether it be churl or chaplain who rides past the chapel,
Monk or priest between masses, or any other man,
He would as soon kill him as go on living.
So I say to you as surely as you sit in your saddle,
Go there and you will be killed, you can be sure of that,
Take my word for it, even if you had twenty lives
      to spend.

He hatz wonyd here ful ȝore,
On bent much baret bende,                                    2115
Aȝayn his dyntez sore
Ȝe may not yow defende.

'Forþy, goude Sir Gawayn, let þe gome one,
And gotz away sum oþer gate, vpon Goddez halue!
Cayrez bi sum oþer kyth, þer Kryst mot yow spede,          2120
And I schal hyȝ me hom aȝayn, and hete yow fyrre
Þat I schal swere bi God and alle his gode halȝez,
As help me God and þe halydam, and oþez innoghe,
Þat I schal lelly yow layne, and lance neuer tale
Þat euer ȝe fondet to fle for freke þat I wyst.'          2125
'Grant merci', quoþ Gawayn, and gruchyng he sayde:
'Wel worth þe, wyȝe, þat woldez my gode,
And þat lelly me layne I leue wel þou woldez.
Bot helde þou hit neuer so holde, and I here passed,
Founded for ferde for to fle, in fourme þat þou tellez,   2130
I were a knyȝt kowarde, I myȝt not be excused.
Bot I wyl to þe chapel, for chaunce þat may falle,
And talk wyth þat ilk tulk þe tale þat me lyste,
Worþe hit wele oþer wo, as þe wyrde lykez
        hit hafe.                                          2135
        Þaȝe he be a sturn knape
        To stiȝtel, and stad with staue,
        Ful wel con Dryȝtyn schape
        His seruauntez for to saue.'

'Mary!' quoþ þat oþer mon, 'now þou so much spellez,       2140
Þat þou wylt þyn awen nye nyme to þyseluen,
And þe lyst lese þy lyf, þe lette I ne kepe.
Haf here þi helme on þy hede, þi spere in þi honde,

A long time he has lived there
And with many has fought.
Do not hope to counter
A death blow like that.

So, good Gawain, let the creature alone,
And go away, in the name of God, by another road.
Ride through some other land, and may Christ take care of you,
And I shall take myself home again, and promise you besides
That I shall swear by God and all his good saints
As God may help me, and the holy relic, and any other oath,
That I shall keep your secret and never tell anyone
That you ever fled for fear of anyone that I know of."
"My thanks to you," Gawain said, and went on impatiently.
"Good fortune to you, man, for your concern about me,
And I believe you would keep my secret,
But though you never spoke of it, if I turned back now,
Running away out of fear, just as you say,
I would be a cowardly knight and nothing could excuse me.
But I will go to the chapel, whatever may happen there
And say what I have to say to that same man,
Whether it turns out well or ill, at the will
        of fate.
            Grim fellow though he may be
            To deal with, and his club, waiting,
            God knows how to find a way
            To save those who do his bidding."

"Mary," said the other man, "now that you spell it all out
And have made up your mind to bring harm upon yourself
And mean to lose your life, I will not stand in your way.
Here is the helmet for your head, your spear in your hand.

And ryde me doun þis ilk rake bi ȝon rokke syde,
Til þou be broȝt to þe boþem of þe brem valay;   2145
Þenne loke a littel on þe launde, on þi lyfte honde,
And þou schal se in þat slade þe self chapel,
And þe borelych burne on bent þat hit kepez.
Now farez wel, on Godez half, Gawayn þe noble!
For alle þe golde vpon grounde I nolde go wyth þe,   2150
Ne bere þe felaȝschip þurȝ þis fryth on fote fyrre.'
Bi þat þe wyȝe in þe wod wendez his brydel,
Hit þe hors with þe helez as harde as he myȝt,
Lepez hym ouer þe launde, and leuez þe knyȝt þere
   al one.   2155
   'Bi Goddez self,' quoþ Gawayn,
   'I wyl nauþer grete ne grone;
   To Goddez wylle I am ful bayn,
   And to hym I haf me tone.'


Thenne gyrdez he to Gryngolet, and gederez þe rake,
Schowuez in bi a schore at a schaȝe syde,   2161
Ridez þurȝ þe roȝe bonk ryȝt to þe dale;
And þenne he wayted hym aboute, and wylde hit hym þoȝt,
And seȝe no syngne of resette bisydez nowhere,
Bot hyȝe bonkkez and brent vpon boþe halue,   2165
And ruȝe knokled knarrez with knorned stonez;
Þe skwez of þe scowtes skayned hym þoȝt.
Þenne he houed, and wythhylde his hors at þat tyde,
And ofte chaunged his cher þe chapel to seche:
He seȝ non suche in no syde, and selly hym þoȝt,   2170
Saue, a lyttel on a launde, a lawe as hit were;
A balȝ berȝ bi a bonke þe brymme bysyde,
Bi a forȝ of a flode þat ferked þare;
Þe borne blubred þerinne as hit boyled hade.

Now ride down this same path around the side of the rock there
Until you come out at the bottom of the wild valley.
Then look a little way off across the meadow on your left
And you will see the Green Chapel in the hollow there,
And the giant who guards it, out in the field.
Now farewell, in God's name, noble Gawain!
For all the gold in the world I would not go with you,
Nor keep you company through this forest one foot farther."
At that the knight in the woods picked up his bridle,
Hit his horse with his heels as hard as he could,
And he leapt across the ground, leaving the other knight there
      alone.
    "By God's self," Gawain said,
    "I will neither wail nor groan.
    I bow to the will of God,
    To whom I have gone."

Then he puts spur to Gryngolet and picks up the path,
Follows along a cliffside at the edge of a small wood,
Rides over the rough hill all the way to the hollow,
And then he looked around him and saw it was a wild place
With no sign of a shelter to be seen anywhere,
But steep banks high above him on both sides,
And rough jagged crags with splintered stones.
He thought the high rocks must be grazing the clouds.
Then he halted, and reined in his horse at that time,
And looked around him everywhere for the chapel.
He saw no such thing and it seemed strange to him.
Then off in an open glade he saw what might be a mound,
A rise like a little hill, on a slope by the water's edge
Where the stream overflowed in a waterfall.
The brook bubbled at the base as though it were boiling.

Þe knyȝt kachez his caple, and com to þe lawe, 2175
Liȝtez doun luflyly, and at a lynde tachez
Þe rayne and his riche with a roȝe braunche.
Þenne he boȝez to þe berȝe, aboute hit he walkez,
Debatande with hymself quat hit be myȝt.
Hit hade a hole on þe ende and on ayþer syde, 2180
And ouergrowen with gresse in glodes anywhere,
And al watz holȝ inwith, nobot an olde caue,
Or a creuisse of an olde cragge, he couþe hit noȝt deme
      with spelle.
        'We! Lorde,' quoþ þe gentyle knyȝt, 2185
        'Wheþer þis be þe grene chapelle?
        Here myȝt aboute mydnyȝt
        Þe dele his matynnes telle!

'Now iwysse,' quoþ Wowayn, 'wysty is here;
Þis oritore is vgly, with erbez ouergrowen; 2190
Wel bisemez þe wyȝe wruxled in grene
Dele here his deuocioun on þe deuelez wyse.
Now I fele hit is þe fende, in my fyue wyttez,
Þat hatz stoken me þis steuen to strye me here.
Þis is a chapel of meschaunce, þat chekke hit bytyde! 2195
Hit is þe corsedest kyrk þat euer I com inne!'
With heȝe helme on his hede, his launce in his honde,
He romez vp to þe roffe of þe roȝ wonez.
Þene herde he of þat hyȝe hil, in a harde roche
Biȝonde þe broke, in a bonk, a wonder breme noyse, 2200
Quat! hit clatered in þe clyff, as hit cleue schulde,
As one vpon a gryndelston hade grounden a syþe.
What! hit wharred and whette, as water at a mulne;
What! hit rusched and ronge, rawþe to here.

The knight urges his horse on and comes to the mound,
Alights gracefully and hitches the reins
To a linden, tying his horse to a thick branch.
Then he turns to the mound and walks around it,
Wondering to himself what it might be.
It had a hole at the end and on either side,
And thick matted grass had grown all over it.
And inside it was all hollow, only an old cave
Or a crevice of an old crag, he could not
        be sure.
          "Oh Lord," said the noble knight,
          "Is this the Green Chapel, then?
          Here I might find, around midnight,
          The devil saying his matins."

*heavy nature imagery*

"Indeed," Gawain said, "this is a desolate spot.
This oratory is ugly with the weeds all over it.
It seems the right place for that knight in green
To perform his devotions in the devil's fashion.
Now in my five wits I feel it is the fiend
Who has trapped me with this tryst to destroy me here.
This is a chapel of ill omen, may an ill fate befall it!
It is the most cursèd church that ever I came into!"
With his helmet on his head, his lance in his hand,
He makes his way up to the wall of that rough lodging.
Then he heard from that high hill, from around a crag
Beyond the brook, on the cliffside, a loud, strange sound.
What! It echoed in the cliff as though it would break it apart,
Like the sound of someone grinding a scythe on a grindstone.
What! It whirred and ground like water turning a mill.
What! It rushed and rang and was painful to hear.

Þenne 'Bi Godde,' quoþ Gawayn, 'þat gere, as I trowe,      2205
Is ryched at þe reuerence me, renk, to mete
        bi rote.
    Let God worche! "We loo"—
    Hit helppez me not a mote.
    My lif þaȝ I forgoo,      2210
    Drede dotz me no lote.'


Thenne þe knyȝt con calle ful hyȝe:
'Who stiȝtlez in þis sted me steuen to holde?
For now is gode Gawayn goande ryȝt here.
If any wyȝe oȝt wyl, wynne hider fast,      2215
Oþer now oþer neuer, his nedez to spede.'
'Abyde', quoþ on on þe bonke abouen ouer his hede,
'And þou schal haf al in hast þat I þe hyȝt ones.'
Ȝet he rusched on þat rurde rapely a þrowe,
And wyth quettyng awharf, er he wolde lyȝt;      2220
And syþen he keuerez bi a cragge, and comez of a hole,
Whyrlande out of a wro wyth a felle weppen,
A denez ax nwe dyȝt, þe dynt with to ȝelde,
With a borelych bytte bende by þe halme,
Fyled in a fylor, fowre fote large—      2225
Hit watz no lasse bi þat lace þat lemed ful bryȝt—
And þe gome in þe grene gered as fyrst,
Boþe þe lyre and þe leggez, lokkez and berde,
Saue þat fayre on his fote he foundez on þe erþe,
Sette þe stele to þe stone, and stalked bysyde.      2230
When he wan to þe watter, þer he wade nolde,
He hypped ouer on hys ax, and orpedly strydez,
Bremly broþe on a bent þat brode watz aboute,
      on snawe.

Then "By God," Gawain said, "that din, I suppose,
Was arranged in my honor as a kind
        of greeting.
    Well, God's will be done.
    Nothing will help me.
    I must give up my life, then.
    But noise will not frighten me."


Then the knight calls at the top of his voice,
"Who is the lord of this place whom I am to meet here?
For now good Gawain is walking right here.
If anyone wants something of him, let him come here at once
Or never after, to get on with what he wants."
"Wait there," someone said on the hill above his head,
"And you shall soon have what I once promised you."
Yet he went on with that rushing noise for a while
And the sound of sharpening, before he would come down.
Then from behind a crag he comes, out of a cave,
Whirling from his hiding place with a gruesome weapon,
A Danish ax, new-made, for dealing the blow,
With a massive blade curving back toward the shaft,
Filed with a whetstone, four feet long, no less,
To judge by the length of its shining thong.
And the knight was dressed as before, all in green,
Green his face and legs, his long hair and his beard,
But now he strides forward, setting his feet down hard.
He held the handle toward the ground and stalked beside it.
When he came to the water he would not wade across.
He vaulted over on his ax and strode on without a break,
His manner menacing, to a broad open space covered
        with snow.

Sir Gawayn þe kynȝt con mete,
He ne lutte hym noþyng lowe;                    2236
Þat oþer sayde, 'Now, sir swete,
Of steuen mon may þe trowe.'


'Gawayn,' quoþ þat grene gome, 'God þe mot loke!
Iwysse þou art welcom, wyȝe, to my place,         2240
And þou hatz tymed þi trauayl as truee mon schulde,
And þou knowez þe couenauntez kest vus bytwene:
At þis tyme twelmonyth þou toke þat þe falled,
And I schulde at þis Nwe ȝere ȝeply þe quyte.
And we ar in þis valay verayly oure one;          2245
Here ar no renkes vs to rydde, rele as vus likez.
Haf þy helme of þy hede, and haf here þy pay.
Busk no more debate þen I þe bede þenne
When þou wypped of my hede at a wap one.'
'Nay, bi God,' quoþ Gawayn, 'þat me gost lante,   2250
I schal gruch þe no grwe for grem þat fallez.
Bot styȝtel þe vpon on strok, and I schal stonde stylle
And warp þe no wernyng to worch as þe lykez,
            nowhare.'
        He lened with þe nek, and lutte,          2255
        And schewed þat schyre al bare,
        And lette as he noȝt dutte;
        For drede he wolde not dare.


Then þe gome in þe grene grayþed hym swyþe,
Gederez vp hys grymme tole Gawayn to smyte;       2260
With alle þe bur in his body he ber hit on lofte,
Munt as maȝtyly as marre hym he wolde;
Hade hit dryuen adoun as dreȝ as he atled,
Þer hade ben ded of his dynt þat doȝty watz euer.

Sir Gawain went to meet him
And bowed, but not low.
"Now, sweet sir," the other said to him,
"You have come as you promised to."

"Gawain," that Green Knight said, "God save you!
You are welcome indeed, man, to my place,
And you have timed your journey as a true man should,
And you know the agreement that we both made:
At this time twelve months ago you took what fell to you
And I was to repay you promptly at this New Year.
And we are all by ourselves in this valley.
There are no knights to part us here. We may fight as we please.
Take your helmet off your head and receive your payment
With no more resistance than I made to you
When you struck my head off with a single blow."
"No, by God," Gawain said, "who gave me my soul,
I shall grudge you not a grain of the harm to come.
But have your one stroke and I will stay still
And offer you no resistance of any kind,
        work as you will."

> He bent his neck and bowed,
> Baring it, white and naked.
> No sign of fear he showed,
> No cowering with dread.

Then at once the knight in green got ready,
Grasping his grim tool to strike Gawain.
With all the brawn in his body he swung it up high,
Aimed a mighty stroke that would surely be the end of him.
If it had slashed down as hard as he started it,
Gawain would have died of the blow, however bravely.

Bot Gawayn on þat giserne glyfte hym bysyde,　　　　　2265
As hit com glydande adoun on glode hym to schende,
And schranke a lytel with þe schulderes for þe scharp yrne.
Þat oþer schalk wyth a schunt þe schene wythhaldez,
And þenne repreued he þe prynce with mony prowde wordez:
Þou art not Gawayn,' quoþ þe gome, 'þat is so goud halden,　　2270
Þat neuer arȝed for no here by hylle ne be vale,
And now þou fles for ferde er þou fele harmez!
Such cowardise of þat knyȝt cowþe I neuer here.
Nawþer fyked I ne flaȝe, freke, quen þou myntest,
Ne kest no kauelacion in kyngez hous Arthor.　　　　　2275
My hede flaȝ to my fote, and ȝet flaȝ I neuer;
And þou, er any harme hent, arȝez in hert;
Wherfore þe better burne me burde be called
　　　　þerfore.'
　　　Quoþ Gawayn, 'I schunt onez,　　　　　2280
　　　And so wyl I no more;
　　　Bot þaȝ my hede falle on þe stonez,
　　　I con not hit restore.

'Bot busk, burne, bi þi fayth, and bryng me to þe poynt.
Dele to me my destiné, and do hit out of honde,　　　　2285
For I schal stonde þe a strok, and start no more
Til þyn ax haue me hitte: haf here my trawþe.'
'Haf at þe þenne!' quoþ þat oþer, and heuez hit alofte,
And waytez as wroþely as he wode were.
He myntez at hym maȝtyly, bot not þe mon rynez,　　　2290
Withhelde heterly his honde, er hit hurt myȝt.
Gawayn grayþely hit bydez, and glent with no membre,
Bot stode stylle as þe ston, oþer a stubbe auþer
Þat raþeled is in roché grounde with rotez a hundreth.
Þen muryly efte con he mele, þe mon in þe grene:　　　2295

But with the side of his eye Gawain saw the ax coming,
Hurtling on its way toward the ground to destroy him,
And his shoulders shrank a little from the sharp edge.
The other swerved in his stroke and held back the blade.
And then he rebuked the prince with a round of proud words.
"You are not Gawain," the knight said, "whom they praise so highly,
Whom no army ever alarmed on hill or in hollow.
Now you flinch with fear before you feel any hurt.
No one ever told me that knight was such a coward.
I neither flinched nor shrank, man, from your stroke,
Nor offered any objections in King Arthur's house.
My head flew to my feet and yet I never flinched,
And you turn faint-hearted before hurt comes to you,
And so it seems clear that I must be called
       the better knight."
     Gawain said, "I flinched once
     And I will not again.
     But if my head falls on the stones
     I cannot put it back on.

But have at it, knight, by your faith, and bring me to the point.
Deal me my destiny, and do it out of hand,
For I shall stand for your stroke and not flinch again
Until your ax strikes me, here is my word upon it."
"Have at you, then," the other said, and heaves it up high,
His face as fierce as that of a madman.
He aims a heavy blow at him but never touches him,
Withheld his hand suddenly before harm was done.
Gawain stood waiting for the blow, no part of him moving,
Still as a stone or as the stump of a tree
Which a hundred roots have anchored in rocky ground.
Then merrily the man in green says to him,

'So, now þou hatz þi hert holle, hitte me bihous.
Halde þe now þe hyȝe hode þat Arþur þe raȝt,
And kepe þy kanel at þis kest, ȝif hit keuer may.'
Gawayn ful gryndelly with greme þenne sayde:
'Wy! þresch on, þou þro mon, þou þretez to longe;                   2300
I hope þat þi hert arȝe wyth þyn awen seluen.'
'For soþe,' quoþ þat oþer freke, 'so felly þou spekez,
I wyl no lenger on lyte lette þin ernde
          riȝt nowe.'
          Þenne tas he hym stryþe to stryke,                        2305
          And frounsez boþe lyppe and browe;
          No meruayle þaȝ hym myslyke
          Þat hoped of no rescowe.

He lyftes lyȝtly his lome, and let hit doun fayre
With þe barbe of þe bitte bi þe bare nek;
Þaȝ he homered heterly, hurt hym no more                           2311
Bot snyrt hym on þat on syde, þat seuered þe hyde.
Þe scharp schrank to þe flesche þurȝ þe schyre grece,
Þat þe schene blod ouer his schulderes schot to þe erþe;
And quen þe burne seȝ þe blode blenk on þe snawe,                  2315
He sprit forth spenne-fote more þen a spere lenþe,
Hent heterly his helme, and on his hed cast,
Schot with his schulderez his fayre schelde vnder,
Braydez out a bryȝt sworde, and bremely he spekez—
Neuer syn þat he watz burne borne of his moder                    2320
Watz he neuer in þis worlde wyȝe half so blyþe—
'Blynne, burne, of þy bur, bede me no mo!
I haf a stroke in þis sted withoute stryf hent,
And if þow rechez me any mo, I redyly schal quyte,
And ȝelde ȝederly aȝayn—and þerto ȝe tryst—                       2325
          and foo.

"So now that you have your courage up I must make my stroke.
Uphold the high knighthood that Arthur bestowed on you
And see whether your neck can survive this blow."
Then Gawain was angry and in a rage he said,
"Well, strike then, you fierce fellow. Your threats take too long.
I begin to believe you are afraid of yourself."
"Indeed," that other knight said, "you speak so boldly,
I will not leave your mission unfulfilled
            any longer."

      Then he plants his feet to strike
      With set mouth and frowning brow.
      What was there for him to like
      With no hope of rescue?


He raised his weapon swiftly and brought it down with skill
Letting the end of the blade graze the bare neck.
Though he swung it hard, the other was hardly hurt,
A cut on the side that barely broke the skin.
The whetted edge sliced through the white fat to the flesh
So the bright blood rushed over his shoulders to the earth.
And when the knight saw the blood gleaming on the snow
He gave a great leap, more than a spear's length,
Caught up his helmet and set it on his head,
Shrugged the splendid shield onto his shoulders,
Unsheaths a bright sword and shouts his challenge,
And never since he was a boy born of his mother
Had he ever been half so happy in this world.
"Enough of your ax, Knight, aim no more blows at me.
I have stood for your stroke here without resisting it.
If you try another I will repay it promptly,
Returning it here and now, you can count upon it,
      with a vengeance.

Bot on stroke here me fallez—
Þe couenaunt schop ry3t so,
Fermed in Arþurez hallez—
And þerfore, hende, now hoo!'               2330

The haþel heldet hym fro, and on his ax rested,
Sette þe schaft vpon schore, and to þe scharp lened,
And loked to þe leude þat on þe launde 3ede,
How þat do3ty, dredles, deruely þer stondez
Armed, ful a3lez: in hert hit hym lykez.              2335
Þenn he melez muryly wyth a much steuen,
And wyth a rynkande rurde he to þe renk sayde:
'Bolde burne, on þis bent be not so gryndel.
No mon here vnmanerly þe mysboden habbez,
Ne kyd bot as couenaunde at kyngez kort schaped.         2340
I hy3t þe a strok and þou hit hatz, halde þe wel payed;
I relece þe of þe remnaunt of ry3tes alle oþer.
Iif I deliuer had bene, a boffet paraunter
I couþe wroþeloker haf waret, to þe haf wor3t anger.
Fyrst I mansed þe muryly with a mynt one,              2345
And roue þe wyth no rof-sore, with ry3t I þe profered
For þe forwarde þat we fest in þe fyrst ny3t,
And þou trystyly þe trawþe and trwly me haldez,
Al þe gayne þow me gef, as god mon schulde.
Þat oþer munt for þe morne, mon, I þe profered,        2350
Þou kyssedes my clere wyf—þe cossez me ra3tez.
For boþe two here I þe bede bot two bare myntes
          boute scaþe.
     Trwe mon trwe restore,
     Þenne þar mon drede no waþe.                    2355
     At þe þrid þou fayled þore,
     And þerfor þat tappe ta þe.

Only one stroke I owed here.
That was what we agreed
In Arthur's hall, and therefore,
Knight, hold your blade."

The other knight turned away from him and rested on his ax,
Set the shaft toward the ground and leaned on the head
And looked at the prince standing there on the field.
How brave, how fearless, how boldly he stood there,
Armed, daring anything, and in his heart he liked him.
Then he spoke pleasantly in his full voice,
The sound of it ringing out as he said to the knight,
"Bold man, do not be so angry on this field.
No one here has misused you or been unmannerly with you
Beyond the agreement made at the King's court.
If I owed you a stroke, you have it. Consider yourself well paid.
I release you of any other debts.
If I had meant to I might have dealt a blow
Far more deadly than that, and done you more harm.
First I made the motion of striking, but it was not serious,
And I left your skin untouched, which was only right,
According to the agreement we made that first night
Which you observed faithfully, keeping your word with me,
Giving me all your gains as a good man should.
The second time I made the motion, man, was for the morning
When you kissed my fair wife. You returned the kisses.
For both of those I offered you only two harmless
      gestures.
   True men pay truly.
   Then they have nothing to fear.
   You failed at number three
   Which you got the cut for.

*[handwritten annotation: theme of exchanging both here and @ castle]*

'For hit is my wede þat þou werez, þat ilke wouen girdel,
Myn owen wyf hit þe weued, I wot wel for soþe.
Now know I wel þy cosses, and þy costes als,     2360
And þe wowyng of my wyf: I wroȝt hit myseluen.
I sende hir to asay þe, and sothly me þynkkez
On þe fautlest freke þat euer on fote ȝede;
As perle bi þe quite pese is of prys more,
So is Gawayn, in god fayth, bi oþer gay knyȝtez.     2365
Bot here yow lakked a lyttel, sir, and lewté yow wonted;
Bot þat watz for no wylyde werke, ne wowyng nauþer,
Bot for ȝe lufed your lyf; þe lasse I yow blame.'
Þat oþer stif mon in study stod a gret whyle,
So agreued for greme he gryed withinne;     2370
Alle þe blode of his brest blende in his face,
Þat al he schrank for schome þat þe schalk talked.
Þe forme worde vpon folde þat þe freke meled:
'Corsed worth cowarddyse and couetyse boþe!
In yow is vylany and vyse þat vertue disstryez.'     2375
Þenne he kaȝt to þe knot, and þe kest lawsez,
Brayde broþely þe belt to þe burne seluen:
'Lo! þer þe falssyng, foule mot hit falle!
For care of þy knokke cowardyse me taȝt
To acorde me with couetyse, my kynde to forsake,     2380
Þat is larges and lewté þat longez to knyȝtez.
Now am I fawty and falce, and ferde haf ben euer
Of trecherye and vntrawþe: boþe bityde sorȝe
       and care!
     I biknowe yow, knyȝt, here stylle,
     Al fawty is my fare;     2386
     Letez me ouertake your wylle
     And efte I schal be ware.'

For that braided belt you are wearing belongs to me.
My own wife gave it to you; I know the story
About your kisses and everything that you did,
And the wooing of my wife. I planned the whole thing.
I sent her to test you, and I am convinced now
That you must be the most perfect knight ever to walk the earth.
As a pearl is more precious than white peas around it,
So, in good faith, is Gawain among other fine knights.
But here you lacked a little, sir, and failed to keep faith,
Though not from treachery, nor my wife's wooing either,
But for love of your life, and I blame you less for that." —→ *wanted to*
That other brave man stood for a long time in thought,            *live too*
So mortified that it cried out inside him.                         *much*
All the blood in his breast pressed into his face
As he shrank back in shame at what the man said.
The first thing that the knight managed to say
Was, "A curse upon cowardice, and coveting too,
For the villainy and vice in them that ruin virtue."
Then he takes hold of the knot and pulls it loose
And in a fury flings it toward the knight.
"Here, take the treacherous thing, and bad luck to it.
From the fear of your stroke, cowardice taught me
To come to terms with coveting, forsaking my own nature
And the openness and good faith that belong to knighthood.
Now I am guilty and a liar, who was always
In dread of disloyalty and lies. Sorrow and grief
          take them both!
     I confess to you, Knight, here between us,
     That what I did was all wrong.
     Let me win back your good grace
     And then heed what I am doing."

Thenn loȝe þat oþer leude and luflyly sayde:
'I halde hit hardily hole, þe harme þat I hade.                                   2390
Þou art confessed so clene, beknowen of þy mysses,
And hatz þe penaunce apert of þe poynt of myn egge,
I halde þe polysed of þat plyȝt, and pured as clene
As þou hadez neuer forfeted syþen þou watz fyrst borne;
And I gif þe, sir, þe gurdel þat is golde-hemmed,                                  2395
For hit is grene as my goune. Sir Gawayn, ȝe maye
Þenk vpon þis ilke þrepe, þer þou forth þryngez
Among prynces of prys, and þis a pure token
Of þe chaunce of þe grene chapel at cheualrous knyȝtez.
And ȝe schal in þis Nwe ȝer aȝayn to my wonez,                                     2400
And we schyn reuel þe remnaunt of þis ryche fest
        ful bene.'
              Þer laþed hym fast þe lorde
              And sayde: 'With my wyf, I wene,
              We schal yow wel acorde,                                             2405
              Þat watz your enmy kene.'


'Nay, for soþe,' quoþ þe segge, and sesed hys helme,
And hatz hit of hendely, and þe haþel þonkkez,
'I haf soiorned sadly; sele yow bytyde,
And he ȝelde hit yow ȝare þat ȝarkkez al menskes!                                 2410
And comaundez me to þat cortays, your comlych fere,
Boþe þat on and þat oþer, myn honoured ladyez,
Þat þus hor knyȝt wyth hor kest han koyntly bigyled.
Bot hit is no ferly þaȝ a fole madde,
And þurȝ wyles of wymmen be wonen to sorȝe,                                        2415
For so watz Adam in erde with one bygyled,
And Salamon with fele sere, and Samson eftsonez—
Dalyda dalt hym hys wyrde—and Dauyth þerafter

Then the other lord laughed and said to him pleasantly,
"I am thoroughly healed of any harm I suffered.
You have confessed so completely, acknowledging your failings,
And you have suffered your penance at the edge of my blade,
I hold you as clear of that offense, and purged as clean,
As though you had made no mistake ever since you were born.
And I give you, sir, the belt with the gold hem around it,
For it is as green as my gown. Sir Gawain, it may
Remind you of this meeting, when you go out again
Among the fine princes, for it is a pure token
Of the adventure of the Green Chapel, for those chivalrous knights.
And in this New Year you shall come again to my house
And we shall celebrate the rest of this holiday
            in joy."
        Then the lord laughed aloud, saying,
        "With my wife, certainly
        You will get along,
        Who once was your enemy."


"No, truly," the knight said, and seized his helmet
Lifting it off politely to thank the other.
"I have stayed as long as I should. Good fortune be with you,
And may he who ordains all honors honor you.
And commend me to your courteous, beautiful wife,
Both to her and the other one, my honored ladies,
Who caught their knight neatly with their cunning.
But it is no wonder if a fool's wits are turned
And he is brought to sorrow by a woman's ways,
For so was Adam beguiled by one on earth,
And Solomon by several of them, and Samson also—
Delilah dealt him his fate—and David afterward

Watz blended with Barsabe, þat much bale þoled.
Now þese were wrathed wyth her wyles, hit were a wynne huge 2420
To luf hom wel, and leue hem not, a leude þat couþe.
For þes wer forne þe freest, þat folȝed alle þe sele
Exellently of alle þyse oþer, vnder heuenryche
   þat mused;
  And alle þay were biwyled      2425
  With wymmen þat þay vsed.
  Þaȝ I be now bigyled,
  Me þink me burde be excused.


'Bot your gordel', quoþ Gawayn, 'God yow forȝelde!
Þat wyl I welde wyth guod wylle, not for þe wynne golde,  2430
Ne þe saynt, ne þe sylk, ne þe syde pendaundes,
For wele ne for worchyp, ne for þe wlonk werkkez,
Bot in syngne of my surfet I schal se hit ofte,
When I ride in renoun, remorde to myseluen
Þe faut and þe fayntyse of þe flesche crabbed,   2435
How tender hit is to entyse teches of fylþe;
And þus, quen pryde schal me pryk for prowes of armes,
Þe loke to þis luf-lace schal leþe my hert.
Bot on I wolde yow pray, displeses yow neuer:
Syn ȝe be lorde of þe ȝonder londe þer I haf lent inne  2440
Wyth yow wyth worschyp—þe wyȝe hit yow ȝelde
Þat vphaldez þe heuen and on hyȝ sittez—
How norne ȝe yowre ryȝt nome, and þenne no more?'
'Þat schal I telle þe trwly,' quoþ þat oþer þenne,
'Bertilak de Hautdesert I hat in þis londe.    2445
Þurȝ myȝt of Morgne la Faye, þat in my hous lenges,
And koyntyse of clergye, bi craftes wel lerned,
Þe maystrés of Merlyn mony hatz taken—

Was beguiled by Bathsheba and it brought him much grief.
As all these were undone by their wiles, it would be far better
To love women without believing them, if ever a man could.
For these, in the old days, were the noblest, whom fortune favored
Above all others under the realm of heaven, and they were
               bemused by love,
        And they were all led astray
        By women they had known.
        If that has happened to me
        Perhaps I may be forgiven.

But your belt," Gawain said, "God reward you for it!
I will be glad to wear it, not for the gold on it,
Nor the sash itself, nor the silk, nor the pendants around it,
Nor its value, nor the honor in it, nor the glorious workmanship,
But I shall look at it often to remind me of my wrongdoing,
When I ride in triumph remorse will recall to me
My failing, and the frailty of wayward flesh,
How easily it is splashed with stains that defile it.
And so when pride from prowess at arms stirs me,
The sight of this love token will humble my heart.
But I ask you one favor, if it does not displease you:
Since you are the lord of the country where I have stayed a while
And have been honored by you—may you be rewarded
By him who holds up the heaven and sits on high—
What is your right name, and I will ask nothing more?"
"I will tell you that certainly," the other said then.
"I am known as Bercilak of the High Desert.
Through the powers of Morgan Le Fay, who lives in my castle,
The subtlety of her lore, the crafts she has made her own,
The many arts of Merlin that she has acquired—

For ho hatz dalt drwry ful dere sumtyme
With þat conable klerk, þat knowes alle your kny3tez          2450
        at hame;
      Morgne þe goddes
      Þerfore hit is hir name:
      Weldez non so hy3e hawtesse
      Þat ho ne con make ful tame—          2455


'Ho wayned me vpon þis wyse to your wynne halle
For to assay þe surquidré, 3if hit soth were
Þat rennes of þe grete renoun of þe Rounde Table;
Ho wayned me þis wonder your wyttez to reue,
For to haf greued Gaynour and gart hir to dy3e
With glopnyng of þat ilke gome þat gostlych speked          2461
With his hede in his honde bifore þe hy3e table.
Þat is ho þat is at home, þe auncian lady;
Ho is euen þyn aunt, Arþurez half-suster,
Þe duches do3ter of Tyntagelle, þat dere Vter after          2465
Hade Arþur vpon, þat aþel is nowþe.
Þerfore I eþe þe, haþel, to com to þyn aunt,
Make myry in my hous; my meny þe louies,
And I wol þe as wel, wy3e, bi my faythe,
As any gome vnder God for þy grete trauþe.'          2470
And he nikked hym naye, he nolde bi no wayes.
Þay acolen and kyssen and kennen ayþer to oþer
To þe prynce of paradise, and parten ry3t þere
        on coolde;
      Gawayn on blonk ful bene          2475
      To þe kyngez bur3 buskez bolde,
      And þe kny3t in þe enker-grene
      Whiderwarde-so-euer he wolde.

For she gave her love tenderly, at one time,
To that greatest of wizards, whom all your knights at home
        have heard of,
    So Morgan the Goddess
    Became her name;
    There is no power one can possess
    That she cannot tame—

She sent me off in that form to your noble hall
To put its pride to the proof and see whether they were true,
The great things that were told of the Round Table.
She put that shape on me to deprive you of your wits
And to grieve Guenever and frighten her to death *jst a social*
With dread of the ghostly way that creature spoke *experiment*
With his head in his hand before the high table.
That is who the ancient lady is at the castle.
She is your own aunt, Arthur's half-sister,
The daughter of the Duchess of Tintagel, who bore Arthur
To belovèd King Uther, and to such honor now.
And so I beg you, Knight, to come visit your aunt.
Celebrate in my house. My men are fond of you,
And like you as well, Knight, upon my word,
As any man under God, for the way you keep your word."
But Gawain said no, by no means would he come.
They embraced and kissed and commended each other
To the Prince of Paradise, and there they parted
      on the cold ground.
    On his fine horse Gawain
    Set off for the castle of the King,
    And the knight in bright green
    Wherever he was going.

Wylde wayez in þe worlde Wowen now rydez

On Gryngolet, þat þe grace hade geten of his lyue;    2480

Ofte he herbered in house and ofte al þeroute,

And mony aventure in vale, and venquyst ofte,

Þat I ne ty3t at þis tyme in tale to remene.

Þe hurt watz hole þat he hade hent in his nek,

And þe blykkande belt he bere þeraboute    2485

Abelef as a bauderyk bounden bi his syde,

Loken vnder his lyfte arme, þe lace, with a knot,

In tokenyng he watz tane in tech of a faute.

And þus he commes to þe court, kny3t al in sounde.

Þer wakned wele in þat wone when wyst þe grete    2490

Þat gode Gawayn watz commen; gayn hit hym þo3t.

Þe kyng kyssez þe kny3t, and þe whene alce,

And syþen mony syker kny3t þat so3t hym to haylce,

Of his fare þat hym frayned; and ferlyly he telles,

Biknowez alle þe costes of care þat he hade,    2495

Þe chaunce of þe chapel, þe chere of þe kny3t,

Þe luf of þe ladi, þe lace at þe last.

Þe nirt in þe nek he naked hem schewed

Þat he la3t for his vnleuté at þe leudes hondes

          for blame.    2500

        He tened quen he schulde telle,

        He groned for gref and grame;

        Þe blod in his face con melle,

        When he hit schulde schewe, for schame.


'Lo! lorde,' quoþ þe leude, and þe lace hondeled,    2505

'Þis is þe bende of þis blame I bere in my nek,

Þis is þe laþe and þe losse þat I la3t haue

Of couardise and couetyse þat I haf ca3t þare;

Þis is þe token of vntrawþe þat I am tan inne,

Now Gawain rides the wild ways of the world
On Gryngolet, when his life had been granted him by grace.
Often he put up in houses and often in the open,
Had many adventures on the way, overcame many,
Which I do not intend to tell you about at this time.
The wound he had in his neck was all healed,
And he wore the shining belt around him
Slanting down to the side like a baldric
With the thong knotted under his left arm
In token of his fault and the stain of it.
And so he comes to the court, whole and unharmed.
Joy woke in that household when the King heard
That good Gawain had come. They were happy to hear it.
The King kisses the knight, and the Queen too,
And many other knights are eager to welcome him,
Asking how he had fared, and he told them the strange story,
Admitting all the hardships he had endured,
What had happened at the Chapel, how the knight acted there,
The love of the lady, and the belt last.
He showed the scar of the wound on his neck
That he had from the knight's hand as a mark of blame
for his bad faith.
He suffered at having to tell it.
Grief and remorse made him groan.
The blood made his face hot
At the shame of making it known.

*And yet he does the right thing in telling it :)*

"Look, sire," he said, and held up the belt,
"This ribbon belongs with the blame branded around my neck,
This is the harm and loss that I endured
For the cowardice and coveting that I was caught in there.
This is the token of the untruth I was taken in

And I mot nedez hit were wyle I may last;                    2510
For mon may hyden his harme, bot vnhap ne may hit,
For þer hit onez is tachched twynne wil hit neuer.'
Þe kyng comfortez þe knyȝt, and alle þe court als
Laȝen loude þerat, and luflyly acorden
Þat lordes and ladis þat longed to þe Table,                  2515
Vche burne of þe broþerhede, a bauderyk schulde haue,
A bende abelef hym aboute of a bryȝt grene,
And þat, for sake of þat segge, in swete to were.
For þat watz acorded þe renoun of þe Rounde Table,
And he honoured þat hit hade euermore after,                 2520
As hit is breued in þe best boke of romaunce.
Þus in Arthurus day þis aunter bitidde,
Þe Brutus bokez þerof beres wyttenesse;
Syþen Brutus, þe bolde burne, boȝed hider fyrst,
After þe segge and þe asaute watz sesed at Troye,            2525
            iwysse,
        Mony aunterez here-biforne
        Haf fallen suche er þis.
        Now þat bere þe croun of þorne,
        He bryng vus to his blysse! AMEN.                     2530


HONY SOYT QUI MAL PENCE.

And I must wear it as long as I live,
For no one can hide the wrong he does, nor be free of it,
For if ever it takes hold, nothing can cut it away."
The king comforts the knight, and all the court also,
And they laughed loudly about it, and agreed, out of friendship,
That the lords and ladies who belonged to the Table,
(Each knight of the brotherhood, should have a baldric,
A bright green sash at a slant around him
Worn for the sake of the knight, the way he did.    *get you*
So it became part of the fame of the Round Table,)    *a squad*
And was an honor forever after to whoever wore it,
And is written in the best book of romance.
Thus in the days of Arthur this adventure came to pass.
The books about Brutus bear witness to this
After Brutus, the bold knight, came here at the beginning
When the siege and the assault on Troy were finished
      indeed.
        Many adventures like this one
        Happened in the days before us.
        May he who bore the crown of thorn
        Bring us to his bliss.


    HONY SOYT QUI MAL PENCE.

## A NOTE ABOUT THE AUTHOR

W. S. Merwin was born in New York City and grew up in Union City, New Jersey, and Scranton, Pennsylvania. From 1949 to 1951 he worked as a tutor in France, Portugal, and Majorca. He has since lived in many parts of the world, most recently on Maui in the Hawaiian Islands, where he cultivates rare and endangered palm trees. His many works of poetry, prose, and translation are listed at the beginning of this volume. He has been awarded a Fellowship of the Academy of American Poets (of which he is a former chancellor), the Pulitzer Prize, and the Bollingen Prize. Most recently, he has received the Governor's Award for Literature of the State of Hawaii, the Tanning Prize for mastery in the art of poetry, a Lila Wallace–Reader's Digest Writers' Award, and the Ruth Lilly Poetry Prize.

## A NOTE ON THE TYPE

This book was set in Junius, a revival of a "Saxon" typeface used by the Clarendon Press and named for Franciscus Junius the younger (1589–1677). Junius was a German philologist and librarian who donated a collection of Gothic, Runic, Icelandic, and Saxon characters to Oxford University. This version of Junius was adapted by Peter S. Baker of the University of Virginia.

Composed by Creative Graphics, Allentown, Pennsylvania
Printed and bound by R. R. Donnelley & Sons,
Harrisonburg, Virginia
Designed by Peter A. Andersen